SCHOOLPROOF

OTHER CROSSWAY BOOKS BY MARY PRIDE

The Way Home

All the Way Home

The Big Book of Home Learning (four volumes)

> *Volume I—Getting Started*
> *Volume II—Preschool and Elementary*
> *Volume III—Teen and Adult*
> *Volume IV—Afterschooling and Enrichment*

The Child Abuse Industry

Unholy Sacrifices of the New Age (with Paul deParrie)

Ancient Empires of the New Age (with Paul deParrie)

Mary Pride

Crossway Books • Westchester, Illinois
A Division of Good News Publishers

Linotronic® Typesetting by TRC Enterprises, 10871
Sunset Hills Plaza, St. Louis, Missouri 63127.

Third printing, 1989

Printed in the United States of America.

Library of Congress Catalog Card Number 87-72953

ISBN 0-89107-480-5

TABLE OF CONTENTS

ACKNOWLEDGMENTS

I owe a very great debt of gratitude to two writers who, I believe, have laid the foundation for a truly Christian education that treats students like people:

- Susan Schaeffer Macaulay, author of *For the Children's Sake*, a presentation and up-to-date application of the program and philosophy of the early nineteenth-century British educator Charlotte Mason.

- Ruth Beechick, author of *A Biblical Psychology of Learning*.

When I discovered these books, I felt like a footsore and weary desert traveler who has just been offered a lift in a brand-new Mercedes. Maybe now I would survive long enough to make it to that lovely educational oasis glimmering faintly in the distance!

In a slightly different way, I also owe many thanks to cleaning expert and philosopher Don Aslett, whose book *Clutter's Last Stand* inspired me to look into the problem of *educational* clutter.

ACKNOWLEDGMENTS

Other thinkers whose works (in my opinion) have raised good questions or supplied good answers include Aristotle, Samuel Blumenfeld, Allan Bloom, the Church Fathers and those who crafted the medieval system of education, Richard Fugate, John Holt, C. S. Lewis, Jerry Manders, my father Dr. Stuart Martin, William McGuffey, Richard Mitchell, Maria Montessori, Raymond and Dorothy Moore, Plato, Diane Ravitch and Chester Finn, Jr., Dorothy Sayers, Edith Schaeffer, Francis Schaeffer, Franky Schaeffer, Socrates, Nancy Wallace, and Marie Winn. Some of these writers touch only tangentially on education, others deal with it substantially; some are quoted in this book, others are not; but all have contributed in some practical way to our own family's education.

Give the Devil his due: B. F. Skinner, Sigmund Freud, Georg Friedrich Hegel, John Dewey, Horace Mann, the NEA and the other great pioneers of manipulative education and cultural illiteracy also deserve some (dubious) credit for making this book necessary.

The questions, applications, and conclusions in this book are, of course, my own responsibility. I disagree on various points with some of the worthies above, and they do (or would, if they were alive to defend themselves) disagree with me. All I can do is gather the best together, stir the soup, and invite you to taste!

INTRODUCTION

I n the best and most popular children's books, children almost never go to school. That is a fact. Think of C. S. Lewis' *Narnia* series, where the action only really starts when the children leave school, and even our own world, behind. Or think of *Alice in Wonderland,* the *Borrowers* series, the early *Little House on the Prairie* books, or *Huckleberry Finn.* Encyclopedia Brown is never seen inside a classroom. The Hardy Boys solve nearly all their mysteries on summer vacation. Nancy Drew never sits behind a school desk. Tommy Stubbins, Dr. Doolittle's young assistant, went to Africa and the moon, but never darkened the door of a classroom. Tom Sawyer did go to school— because he had to— but nobody could accuse him of enjoying it. Even the English schoolboy books tended to present school as a necessary evil to be ignored as much as possible, and the few examples of this genre that have survived were the anti-school schoolboy books of Rudyard Kipling (*Stalky and Co.*) and P. G. Wodehouse (*Psmith*).

Maybe those old and new children's books have something to tell us. Children don't automatically trust school: why should we?

INTRODUCTION

I won't bore you with long lists of reasons for having less than perfect trust in our present school system. We all know all about seventeen-year-olds who can't read or write or tell Florida from Mainland China. We are up-to-date with the latest facts about the schoolkid drug problem and the teen suicide epidemic. We aren't even as surprised as we should be to hear on the radio that the school superintendent in Detroit has announced a "tough new policy" of ejecting gun-toting students from his schools (you mean to say that until now they have been allowed to *stay?* and that there are a *lot* of kids with guns in school?) and that the ACLU wants to forbid school officials to search lockers for those guns. The point is, "Why should your children . . . or my children . . . be among the casualties? Why should we take the chance?"

Many people today are admitting that our educational system has gone rather wrong. They propose that we tinker with it to make it better.

I propose that we not wait around for the tinkerers.

We need to take control, *now,* of our own children's education.

This book will show you how to do that.

WHAT IS SCHOOLPROOFING?

Schoolproofing means making sure your children get a great education, no matter what political or educational theory happens to be in vogue. It means having children who learn to read in an age of illiteracy; who learn to obey legitimate authority in an age of sullen rebellion; who learn to stand against injustice in an age of craven conformity. It means that *your* children will be smarter, more affectionate, less dependent on external rewards and punishments. It means that you will be more confident, less worried about your children, more able to enjoy them and have high hopes for their future.

Schoolproofing means learning how to educate, so you can recognize good and bad education. It means knowing your options: different ways of presenting a lesson, different educational philosophies, different types of teaching setups.

Schoolproofing means YOU are in control. You will have the tools to shop around intelligently in the educational marketplace, or even to opt out and do it yourself. You will recognize the warning signs if a change is needed, and have the power to make the change. You will have more respect for good teachers, and less awe of the bad. You will understand your children's difficulties and triumphs.

No longer will your children have to stand in line at the educational cafeteria and take whatever is dished out. You will have learned how to cook up your own educational feasts; and if you choose, instead of doing your own cooking, to send the children to a better restaurant, you will know what to look for.

CAN THIS SCHOOL BE SAVED?

It is wonderful to be able to teach your own children yourself, and I would like to encourage all parents of young children to do this. It is quite another matter to *have* to teach your own children right up through college and beyond, simply because you have no other hope of giving them a truly noble and good education.

So, this book asks another question: need school be the peer-group-dominated, one-size-fits-all, tedious secular mess it is nowadays?

The answer is a resounding *No*. The Christian education movement is already asking some of the right questions; we simply need to add a few more. The last part of this book is an attempt to challenge Christian schools to drop the format, content, and assumptions still carried over from the counter-Christian government schools, and to present a vision of what Christian education (including home schooling) *could* be.

SIMPLE IS BEAUTIFUL

Simple is beautiful. There, if you want it, is the root and sum of my educational philosophy. Knowledge is complex enough, students are complex enough, without making teaching complicated, too.

Where most books on teaching and learning delight in giving you long lists of unique and clever ideas, or at least lots of long words to mull over, here you'll find just the opposite. This book tries to simplify. Instead of sixty-two clever ideas for teaching punctuation and forty-seven nifty science enrichment projects, you will find a manageable number of different ways to present lessons and get feedback on them that apply to *every* subject area. Instead of ideas for creating your own world maps and alphabet-teaching-widgets from leftover pencil stubs and flour paste, I'm going to try to help you organize the stuff you already have— and figure out what among it really belongs in the trash pile. Instead of fifty darling ways to use computers in your home or classroom, we will concentrate on *when* and *if* computers and other electronic media are helpful. Books— in place of lists of creative questions to ask children about particular books, we will think about how to use books to ease your teaching load, and *which* books to use.

Throughout this book, I assume you are the teacher. This makes the book more convenient both to write and to read. But I hope it will have another effect; helping you realize that you CAN teach your own children.

INTRODUCTION

Teaching is not so very mysterious, after all. It may be miraculous, but it is not mysterious. Man plants— that is not mysterious. Man waters— again, no mystery. But God giveth the increase— by a miracle.

PART I

SOMETHING BEAUTIFUL FROM GOD

CHAPTER ONE

ARE STUDENTS HUMAN?

EDUCATION IS (pick one):

❏ *A ticket to a good job.*
❏ *Teachers molding kids to fit them into society.*
❏ *What happens spontaneously when children are left completely free to follow their own interests.*
❏ *Giving people the tools to more fully love and serve God and their neighbor.*
❏ *None of the above.*

Today education has gone to the dogs . . . and the rats, and the pigeons . . . and to the machines. Children are considered animals for teachers to train in the way we train a dog, or computers for teachers to program. As Dr. Ruth Beechick, a woman who has spent a lifetime in the education field, observes,

> Something was always missing [from my university education classes]. In the "rat" classes [behavioral psychology], there was no human will or purpose. In the "couch" classes [humanistic psychology], there was no God or other reality outside the person and his relationships. The books and theories never seemed to describe what I was doing in my own learning and teaching . . .
>
> Behaviorism, for instance, was developed largely from the study of rats, pigeons, and other laboratory animals. And why not? If man is just

as personless as a pigeon, it ought to be good enough to study how pigeons learn and then transfer the principles to teaching people. The major principles in behaviorism concern environment—the stimulus and rewards. Learning is measured by outer responses only. There is no person inside to be concerned with . . .

Humanists sound a little better in their writings. They believe there is something uniquely human about man. . . Man has evolved something or other beyond what animals have . . . But whatever it is, it has biological roots. All we have to do is explain biology in terms of chemistry, then explain chemistry in terms of molecular behavior, and so on down. When we have man reduced to his scientific lowest terms, we will have figured out what is uniquely human about him.[1]

We have to stop right here and not go further until we have figured this out. *Are* students human? Or are they (and we) just machines? If students are human, what does it mean to be human? Does "human" mean just a smarter animal, one further step up the evolutionary latter . . . or do humans have a spiritual side?

SMILEY FACES AND UNCORRECTED PAPERS

These are not remote academic questions. When your Jennifer trots home carrying papers covered with smiley-face stickers and workbooks filled with dozens of dull little drills about tiny little facts, be sure the behaviorists are trying to program Jennifer. If Sammy's teacher refuses to correct his spelling, grammar, and punctuation because Sammy is "learning to express himself creatively," then know that humanists are hoping Sammy will experience some kind of grammar-transcending evolutionary breakthrough. When neither Jennifer nor Sammy knows how to read very well, or cipher very well, and neither can tell you who Nathan Hale was or locate the United States on a plainly-labeled world map, pin the blame where it belongs— on an educational system that refuses to believe children are human.

The Bible says, "God created man in His own image." Your own experience says, "I am a person, not an animal or a machine." All of history screams, "People will live and die for things like justice and religious truth that computers and dogs will never understand." Let behaviorists (with their belief in deterministic programming) explain the American Revolution, or humanists (with their belief in evolutionary progress) explain World War II. They can't. More to the present point, they also can't explain why children, presented with the very cleverest and most up-to-date programming techniques, refuse to obey their behaviorist programmers; and why children, given the opportunity to invent their own civilization from a fresh slate wiped deliberately clean of all our civilization's previous progress, end up looking stupider instead of smarter.

I won't belabor this point any further. It should be clear that the behaviorists and humanists, given free rein, have crippled Western education. The results speak for themselves. Now, what will we do about it?

We know how to program computers. We know how to train dogs. But today we know very little about how to teach human beings. It's time to look at what is special about us as humans, and how humans deserve to be treated.

HAVE A HEART!

In our IQ-happy world, superior brain size is often thought of as the main difference between people and animals. Lack of brain capacity is also increasingly (and wickedly) considered grounds enough for withholding food, water, and genuine education from those so afflicted.

It is more than interesting, then, that, as Ruth Beechick points out, the Bible uses the word "heart" some 800 times and the word "brain" never. The heart is mentioned as a seat of spiritual life, moral life, emotional life, motivations, and even thought life. Moreover, the presence or absence of brain waves is perfectly irrelevant to the Bible's definition of life itself. "The life of the flesh is in the blood," say the Scriptures (Leviticus 17:11, 14), indicating that you are truly dead when your heart stops beating, not when some fancy machine ceases to register brain waves.

If you have jumped to the conclusion that the Bible is just out-of-date in its terminology, since now we *know* that the brain controls all our thinking and learning, you will be as surprised as I was to find out that experimental research now shows the heart "talking" to the brain. Ruth Beechick reports on this research in her book, *A Biblical Psychology of Learning.* As she concludes,

> It is quite acceptable in our times to associate mind with brain, to assume that immaterial mind works through us by using our material brain. It is less acceptable to associate heart with heart, to assume that the age-old immaterial heart functions [love, hate, moral choices, belief and unbelief, meditation] work through us by using our material heart. Time may change that.
>
> But the fact remains that the Bible gives great prominence to heart, and a biblical learning theory cannot ignore that.[2]

If you are not a Christian and all this talk of what the Bible says about "heart" makes you uncomfortable, think about "spirit" instead. Why do human beings desire immaterial concepts like love, freedom, justice, and beauty— sometimes at the cost of our own physical comforts, or even our lives? How can chemical processes impel a man to do something completely against his *natural* urges to comfort and self-preservation? Why, after seventy years of official atheism, are there Christians and Jews in Russia?

MOTIVATION AND MANIPULATION

Our belief, or lack of belief, in the child's human heart will completely determine the way we teach that child. It also determines how we treat adult students and workers.

Let's now look at the possible ways students can be motivated to learn.

The Child as Cog

Here is your classic behaviorist Beyond-Freedom-and-Dignity position. (Eminent behaviorist B. F. Skinner actually wrote a book by that title.) Every tool of manipulation is allowed. Try to smash the child's heart and destroy his personal inclinations. Sterilize and empty the environment; then recreate it, bringing in only the "inputs" you want the child to receive. The teacher is God. The child is a "human resource"— a slave without even the slave's right to resent his slavery.

Charlotte Mason, referring to the "organized, child-centered atmosphere of a pleasant kindergarten," warned us,

> Everything is directed, expected, suggested. No other personality out of book, picture, or song, no, not even that of Nature herself, can get at the children without the mediation of the teacher. No room is left for spontaneity or personal initiation on their part.[3]

Today, most behaviorist-driven environments are not that pleasant, but the same principle still applies. *Everything* is mediated to the student through a controlled source: the teacher, the computer, the textbook. Teachers are controlled by rules that allow administrators to fire them for not following "curriculum guidelines" (but not for homosexual solicitation). Computers are controlled by choice of software. Textbooks are controlled by feminist and one-world-government censorship committees.

Even the lingo of behaviorism is repellent. Inputs. Student outcomes. Communications. Segments. Factors. Learning gradients. The ultimate, desired Student Outcome is a crop of good little robot workers and good little robot welfarites who have learned to support The System.

Let me say right here and now that pasting the word "Christian" on behaviorist robot-molding doesn't make that kind of education Christian. We hear an awful lot about "molding Christian character," an unfortunate phrase that implies children are lumps of beeswax. I also see the glimmerings of a push for "Christian" Early Childhood Education (meaning church baby-sitting programs featuring hours of formal drill). Christian schools sometimes even advertise themselves as behavior-molding institutions, rather like military schools used to. "We will take your disobedient little nuisance and teach him to stand in line and say 'Yes, Ma'am' like a little soldier." That's fine, as long as he also learns to stand against tyranny like a little Revolutionary War patriot or early Roman martyr.

Education means engaging the heart, soul, will, and spirit, not just learning to avoid punishment and grovel for rewards. *Christian* education is supposed to point kids beyond these earthly rewards and punishments altogether. Simply teaching kids to be compliant *no matter what* is not Christian.

The Child as Dog

You hold the lollipop. "Want a lollipop, Judy? Then do ten more arithmetic problems." This is called the Pleasure Principle, and you are role playing an animal trainer. Instead of doggie biscuits, you are offering your little learners smiley-face stickers, candy, and trips to amusement parks.

Something can be said for the Pleasure Principle. For one thing, it doesn't grind the student down like pure behaviorism. You no longer are trying to control the child's total environment, just his lollipop intake. Animal trainers don't worry if their trainees run around freely after the lesson.

The only thing wrong with the Pleasure Principle is that kids are not dogs. The Pleasure Principle, however, teaches them to think like dogs. "Do it for the reward, not for the joy of a task well done. Try to con the teacher into more and better prizes. Sit up and beg. Act cute." Those determined to remain human can only growl and disdain the tempting prizes, thus getting themselves labeled noncooperative or emotionally disturbed.

Vacation Bible Schools routinely fall back on Child-as-Dog motivations. "The winning team will get a trip to the amusement park . . . or toy trains . . . or teddy bears!" "Bring in your memory work and get gold stickers on your card." Why do we do this? Is the Bible *really* so boring that nobody will study it without the incentive of toy trains and trips to Six Flags? Then why do *I* study it when nobody has ever offered to take me to Six Flags? Why do *you*?

The Child as Snob

We have now moved beyond the childish Pleasure Principle to the more adult Glory Principle. Press for Success. Do It Because It Will Make You Rich and Famous (or at least get you a part-time job at Burger King). The motivation we coyly hold out before the student is a long-term result appealing only to his selfishness.

I have complained elsewhere about "character-building" materials that are nothing more than this sort of corrupt appeal to pride and greed. The same goes for all those lectures about "learning this because it will be get you a job, or money, or social status later on." As Susan Schaeffer Macaulay says,

> Perhaps the most widely used method of motivation is to play upon the natural desires of power and ambition. These can and do have their place in every person's life. But they should not be used as a manipulative device. Johnny and Anne have enough to cope with without being positively pushed into feeling pride or failure. Aren't we "all members of one body"? . . . Is it not materialistic to encourage older children to feel that education is *only* useful for passing exams? Especially when we hammer home that these are the passports to higher salaries? Is this why "higher education" is such a failure that the average U. S. college graduate reads only one book a year?[4]

The teacher is now in the position of a flatterer, delighting the child with his prospects in order to bend him to the teacher's will. A villainous role not worthy of you or me.

The Child as God

"What do *you* want to do today, Johnny?"

"Watch TV all day."

"That's lovely, dear. But you've watched TV all day for months. Are you *sure* that's all you want to do?"

"Yep."

"OK, it's your life."

Here you are with no lollipops and no punishments. No fair to use praise or disapproval, either. Your child's word has become law. His freedom is absolute, and no adult may guide, discipline, or instruct him in any way except upon his (the child's) own specific request.

What has happened? You haven't eliminated teacher/student or parent/child roles. You've simply *reversed* them. *You* may apply no motivations to your child, but he is not so constrained. Since his inbuilt desires are presumed to be always good, and since you as parent or "teacher" have the job of serving the child's needs, guess who tells who what to do?

Though the child-as-god view is in the long run a more serious and subtle threat to education than more obvious schemes of manipulation, you are not likely to have too much trouble with it in the public school system, where the opposite view prevails. It crops up more often in "free" or "alternative" schools, and in home schooling circles among New Agers, followers of Rudolf Steiner, and the disciples of John Holt. (John Holt himself had a more balanced and realistic view: see the footnote).[5]

Child-as-god doctrine always *sounds* really wonderful. Let the children alone and they will come home, wagging their tails behind them. With no interference, they will learn just what they need to learn. If they want to watch TV all day, or dig holes in the backyard, or play video games, no need to worry that they are missing out on an education. For some mystical reason they *need* to waste their lives in this fashion. Not only that, but they are really learning something important in this way (though we don't know exactly what!). We don't have to work at teaching them at all. No conflicts, no problems.

I admit that when children really respect their parents (or other adults or children) they are anxious to learn from them. Grandmas and Grandpas can often sidestep the whole question of authority. But children are also foolish and ignorant of how to withstand temptation. The more foolish will often bypass a parent's example— no matter how worthy— in favor of some immediate selfish whim. Pinocchio, as a literary example, really *wanted* to go to Donkey Island instead of to school as his father had requested. Canned entertainment appealed more to Pinocchio than an education— and he is by no means the only student who has ever felt that way. Jiminy Cricket would have done him no favors by leaving him to his own devices.

To put it more Scripturally: Jesus Christ Himself "learned obedience from what He suffered," and He did it *against* the desires of His human nature, in "reverent submission" to His Father (Hebrews 5:8). Submission and obedience are not *bad,* provided you are submitting to a legitimate authority giving a legitimate command. Authority is not necessarily a mindless force beating and breaking down everything in its path. Legitimate authority derives from God's authority, and is accountable to Him (Romans 13:1-2). Inbuilt human desires are not our sole authority.

Because authority comes from God, we are not in the humiliating position of bowing to mere humans. God makes the laws, not men. *God* said, "Thou shalt honor thy father and mother": parents didn't make that up. God also ordered parents not to frustrate their children, to be gentle to them, and to nurture them, among many other positive things. Both adults and children are under the same Law. Thus, the adults can respect the child's humanness without having to worship it, and children can respect the adults in authority over them without becoming slavish.

The Child with a Human Heart

We have seen that since people are not cogs, we may not destroy their spirits by playing God with their environment or behavior. We have also seen that since people are not dogs and should not become snobs, we should not corrupt their spirits by bribing them with selfish motivations; and that since children are not gods, we may not rely solely on their inbuilt motivations.

But if students should not be treated like cogs, dogs, snobs, or gods, what then?

The Apostle Paul, a very wise man, once condensed the goal and means of Christian education into a single sentence. He said, "The goal of this command is love, which comes from a pure heart and a good conscience and a sincere faith" (1 Timothy 1:5).

"The goal of this command . . . " Of what command? Of the sum total of Christian teaching, which Paul was talking about in the previous sentence and returned to in the next. The goal of Christian education is not to produce

• slavish robots (cogs)

• materialistic consumers (dogs)

• selfish glory hounds (snobs)

• or clever Hitlers (gods).

The goal of Christian education is "love." And the Bible's definition of love is

(1) a heart submitted to God ("Thou shalt love the Lord thy God will all thy heart and all thy soul and all thy mind and all thy strength . . . " "If you love Me, you will keep My commandments")

(2) and the heart-desire and ability to serve others ("Thou shalt love thy neighbor as thyself").

Judge for yourself whether or not this is a worthy goal!

MOTIVATIONS DETERMINE YOUR GOAL

Once we know who our students are (Cogs? Dogs? Snobs? Gods? Human beings made in the image of God?) we can finally begin to talk about educational methods. It does no good at all to speak of educating another human being if we have wrong ideas about the goal of education and the means we may use to achieve that goal. Motivations *determine* the goal.

A child manipulated by behaviorists discovers that the goal of his education is to make him into a cog. Carrot-and-stick motivations cannot produce independent thinkers, only well-trained animals. Appeals to pride make children proud. Appeals to greed make them greedy. Refusal to guide and direct children produces children who think they are gods.

If you're with me so far, you agree that our education must have a heart. It must respect the child's spiritual nature without worshiping it. Charlotte Mason put this well when she spoke of "the respect due to the personality of children, which must not be encroached upon, whether by fear or love, suggestion or influence, or undue play upon any one natural desire." She suggested that this means "we are limited to three educational instruments— the atmosphere of ENVIRONMENT, the discipline of HABIT, and the presentation of LIVING IDEAS" (capitals mine).[6]

These motivational tools— the atmosphere of environment, the discipline of habit, and the presentation of living ideas— accord well with the idea of the goal of love attained through "a pure heart, a good conscience, and a sincere faith."

MOTIVATION THAT FITS

You have a right to purify your child's environment. This is completely different from the behaviorist's desire to totally control the environment. Think of the child's environment as an oil painting, and yourself as a landscape painter. It's the painter's privilege to leave an ugly bunch of weeds or unpleasing structure out of his painting. In this way, your picture is actually more real, being closer to the way God created the world. The world, after all, started out "very good" (Genesis 1:31). Behaviorists, in contrast, ignore the landscape of God's creation entirely, preferring to start with a black canvas on which they carefully arrrange man-made geometric forms.

You also have a right, under God, to purify your children's behavior. This does not mean we can use any means we like to force them to be externally good. Our goal is "love"—joy and delight in doing right for its own sake. Towards this end, we will discourage negative habits and encourage good ones, thus building up the child's ability to govern himself. More on this in later chapters.

Finally, *you have a duty to seek out and present the truth to your child.* Sincere faith is not built on sand. It's your job to decide what is important and true enough to be worth the effort of teaching and learning. We should not leave our children to stumble around in the dark. More on this, also, later.

You and I are on the outside of our students. We can't grab hold of their hearts and mold them to fit our whims. For that, let us give thanks. Yet we are not shut out from their hearts, either. We have access to that most sacred portion of their being through love, and through the ministrations of the Holy Spirit—through prayer and faithfulness to God's goal and His appointed means. *Our* motivations are important, too.

Students are human. Human beings, ultimately, must make the effort of learning. You can't *make* me learn . . . but you can teach me the Learning Game. Find out how to play the game in the next chapter.

CHAPTER TWO

THE LEARNING GAME

"You can lead a horse to water, but you can't make him drink."   Old English proverb

"Maybe you can't make a horse drink—but you sure can salt his oats!"   Anonymous American farmer

We know that children aren't horses. After all, we just spent the last chapter proving that children are neither exotic animals to be tamed nor lumps of raw material to be molded. Still, the old proverb about leading a horse to water—and the somewhat more recent proverb about salting his oats—both have something to teach us about teaching.

Picture two horses. The first, dragged to the watering trough by his impatient master, balks and whinnies. He doesn't want to drink right then, perhaps because he is not thirsty, perhaps out of sheer cussedness, sensing his master's haste. The second, thirsty from his meal of salted oats, comes eagerly to the water. No finicky drinker he; not with his raging thirst!

Now, picture two children. The first, dragged to the schoolbooks by his eager teacher, balks and whines. He doesn't want to study right then; perhaps because he just isn't interested, perhaps because he senses that the eagerness is all his teacher's and none of his. The second, with his appetite for learning kindled by previous pleasant learning experiences and a host of unanswered questions that beg for solutions, comes eagerly to the books. No finicky student he; not with his raging curiosity!

What is the difference? The difference between the drinking horse and the finicky horse is that one had salt in his oats. The difference between the studying child and the balking child is that one had "salt in his oats"— he had a taste of learning that made him thirsty for more.

To the real student, learning is not drudgery, even if it involves serious labor. It is meat and drink for his soul. It is, if I may put it this way, a game— the best game of all.

Since we are going to talk about "the game of learning," please don't think of what adults sometimes mean by a game— a pleasant but frivolous contest whose outcome does not (or should not) greatly matter to anyone. Think instead of what a game, of what play, is to a child. Charlotte Mason sums it up so perfectly:

> . . . that quality of spontaneity, imagination, wholehearted concentration, and joy which should mark all children at play.[1]

Spontaneity! Imagination! Wholehearted concentration! Joy! This is what Christians are supposed to bring to *every* task, doing it "wholeheartedly, as unto the Lord, not unto men." In this sense, the most mature Christian is the one who plays best— who becomes "like a little child" in his work and study. C. S. Lewis put it admirably when he said that the greatest Christian is not one who pursues a hated task with dogged devotion, but the one who learns to enjoy the once-hated task for the sake of Jesus Christ.

MRS. PIGGLE-WIGGLE AND THE GAME OF LEARNING

Some people have taken me to task for a what they consider a too-egalitarian view of human ability. They, quite rightly, point out that a genius, by definition, is different from other people. According to them, most children can't possibly be geniuses.

I do recognize that we are all born with a different amount of native quickness. But genius is not only, or primarily, quickness. Ask Thomas Edison. He said that genius was one percent inspiration and ninety-nine percent perspiration. And Thomas Edison should know. He invented the electric light and the phonograph, to name just a few of his contributions. Nobody has ever questioned whether Edison was a genius!

The real question, then, is why do some people perspire and sweat after knowledge, while others don't? The answer is simple— and explains why our present school system produces such an amazing shortfall of genius. *A genius is a person to whom learning is a game.* And we *can* help our children and students discover the game of learning.

Take Mrs. Piggle-Wiggle, for example. This fictional lady, the humpbacked widow of a pirate captain, stars in a series of children's books. Mrs. Piggle-Wiggle is the harassed mother's last resort: a dear little old lady who always knows just what to do to help a child break a bad habit or learn a good one.

In the very first Mrs. Piggle-Wiggle story, in the very first Mrs. Piggle-Wiggle book, Mrs. Piggle-Wiggle confronts a little girl who just *hates* to work.

The little girl's name was Mary Lou Robertson and she was eight years old and quite fat, and she was running away from home. She told Mrs. Piggle-Wiggle all this after she had drunk three cups of cambric tea and eaten seven sugar cookies. She said, "I'm running away from home because I hate to wash dishes. All I do is wash dishes. I am just a servant. Dishes! Dishes! Dishes! Wash, dry, put away. That's all I do. My mother doesn't love me at all. She isn't my real mother, anyway. She probably got me out of an orphanage just to wash her dishes." Mary Lou began to cry again . . .

"Now that's a funny thing," said Mrs. Piggle-Wiggle. "I mean your hating to wash dishes so much, because you see, I like to wash dishes. In fact I enjoy washing dishes so much that a cause of great sorrow to me is the fact that the only dishes I must wash are for Wag, Lightfoot and me. Three or four dishes a meal, that's all.

"When I wash dishes, Mary Lou, I pretend that I am a beautiful princess with long, golden curly hair . . . and apple-blossom skin and forget-me-not blue eyes. I have been captured by a wicked witch and my one chance to get free is to wash every single dish and have the whole kitchen sparkly clean before the clock strikes. For when the clock strikes, the witch will come down and inspect, to see if there is a crumb anywhere. If there are pots and pans that have been put away wet, if the silverware has been thrown in the drawer, or if the sink has not been scrubbed out, the witch will have me in her power for another year."

Mrs. Piggle-Wiggle looked at the clock and jumped up. "It is ten minutes to four, Princess, and we have so much to do. Hurry, hurry, hurry!" [2]

If you are alert (which I wasn't, the first time I read this story), you will notice several things Mrs. Piggle-Wiggle could have done better. For one thing, she focused Mary Lou's attention *away* from her task, rather than showing her how to enjoy the task itself. For another, she fostered a basically slavish attitude towards the work. Instead of working for a mythically hostile mother, Mary Lou ended up working for a deliciously scary old witch. Her only reward was avoiding harm at the hands of the witch. As an improvement, Mary Lou could have pretended that she was a lost princess whose true love could only recognize her by the perfectly spotless dishes she washed. My feeling is that whatever Mary Lou pretended, the game would get pretty old after a few days. Her basic animosity towards dishwashing was not overcome, just distracted.

Yet, Mrs. Piggle-Wiggle's idea was fundamentally sound. Mary Lou needed to learn to enjoy dishwashing.

WHAT SORT OF GAME IS THIS?

The game of learning is not adding on silly activities to serious subjects (like dishwashing and aeronautical engineering). It is *making learning itself a game*– getting absorbed in the problem, the answers, the process of learning. Concretely: it is a child gazing at the pattern of the tiles on her bathroom floor and devising mathematical equations to explain the regularities. It is Galileo watching the pendulum swing back and forth and timing it by his pulse to see if the swings really take the same amount of time no matter how wide they are. It is a boy making "the greatest paper airplane ever," and his younger brother secretly vowing to make a greater one. It is Grandma daringly substituting chicken for hamburger in a favorite recipe to see what will happen. It is the computer hacker hanging around the mainframe in the wee hours for "just one more run" to see if his program will compile and work *this* time. It is all things become new, because they are loved and admired and watched with wonder and a sense of sudden surprise.

What the game of learning is *not* is what Charlotte Mason calls "twaddle." Twaddle is taking a perfectly serious, simple subject and attempting to disguise it with hand puppets, playlets, jingles, blackboard activities, and all the hundred and one ways teachers have been taught to waste our and our students' time. Twaddle is pretending that the marvelously exciting truths of life are ill-tasting potions that need much more than a spoonful of sugar to help them down. Twaddle is insisting that children are too immature for Shakespeare, and giving them instead immortal lines such as, "I am me. You are you. We are not the same"— all accompanied, of course, by colorful props and supplementary handwork. Twaddle is hugely, always, *grownup* twaddle— stuff no self-respecting child would ever invent himself.

Children really do want to grow up and do important, big, adult things. I can still remember the catch in my throat as I saw older girls (oh, how envied) carrying their books carelessly bound with a *real elastic* book strap, and flaunting their beautiful fountain pens. We lowly first- and second-graders had no book straps, and we weren't to be allowed near fountain pens until the Powers That Be were assured we were experts in pencilmanship. I can also remember the awful embarrassment of the kindergarten class where our chirpy teacher instructed us to "wave our little leaves in the breeze." I wanted to play at being a Big Girl with a large load of books and a real fountain pen, not at being a darling little blushing tree among rows of other darling little blushing trees. I do not recall any of my classmates ever suggesting, then or afterward, that we play Little Trees in the Breeze. We did, however, play School and House and Cowboys and Indians— none of which, oddly enough, the chirpy kindergarten teacher ever asked us to play in school.

DO YOU PLAY THE GAME?

One of the great differences between teachers who understand that students are human and teachers who don't, is their relative willingness to do unto others only what they want done unto them. Teachers who think of students as strange beings from another planet find themselves saying things like, "This material is boring, all right . . . but it's *so* good for the children!" A teacher who considers her students interesting raw material to poke and pull into shapes of her choosing doesn't even have to think about whether the lesson work is boring or not. It's just there to be shoveled down, and very likely the teacher has had to munch plenty of it herself in education class. Her motto has become, "Swallow without chewing and you won't notice the flavor."

Nobody likes this. Kids hate studying boring stuff. Teachers hate teaching it. Parents hate reading it aloud. "'Ha, ha, laughed the kitties. Ha, ha, ha, ha.' Good heavens, Janie, do you *really* want me to read this to you to the end?"

Twaddle is twaddle, whether in the small kid-sized packet or the large economy portion. No fair dumping on another what you very sensibly reject yourself! As Charlotte Mason said,

> The adult, whether teacher or parent, has to be able to enjoy and understand what he or she is reading with the children . . . If you share with children the very best, carefully chosen to meet their needs, they will amaze everyone.[3]

Kids need protection from the (probably radioactive) fallout of educational twaddle raining down from the skies. Schoolproofing hint: Ask, "Why is Katy studying this? Why should *anyone* have to study this?" instead of ordering Katy to open wide and swallow another lump of the deadly stuff. If *you* wouldn't touch the book or exercise with a ten-foot pole, trust your good sense. Tell your children, "This is what twaddle looks like," and try to insulate them from it.

THE GAME OF SELF-DISCIPLINE

"What should we do to encourage creativity in our children?" Ruth Beechick asks. Her answer, surprisingly, is "discipline them and encourage self-discipline."

> The advice to be careful about discipline because we might stifle children's natural creativity does not fit the biblical theory of this book. It is discipline which leads to the moral, emotional, and spiritual commitment needed to learn anything creatively or produce anything creative. But this does not mean rigid, conforming classrooms . . Allow them time and freedom for total absorption. . . In children, this absorption may be one of the main things to aim for. Another is helping them experience secondhand the thrill of creation. . . Still a third approach is to aim as much as possible for an understanding level rather than just the knowing level.[4]

Discipline can become a game. It can also be work. It changes from work to a game with practice, as you gain the proper tools and discipline becomes a habit.

A good example of this, at least for me, is writing a book. Writing my first book was a tremendously painful experience. It took me three years, and I wanted to quit at least a hundred times. The manuscript went through twenty drafts, all but the last on an old manual typewriter. What sustained me was the inner conviction that I was supposed to write that book, and the ultimate desire that other people would read it. This is "writing-to-have-written," as writing teacher William Zinsser calls it.

Learning to write has been a process of some years and much labor and study. I have read books on writing and rewritten thousands of pages. But the desire to improve and to communicate keeps me interested in writing and everything surrounding it. I will not say that writing has become positively a game for me—I still prefer reading to writing—but the pain of writing is steadily decreasing Meanwhile, the pleasure of learning about writing has increased, so that learning about writing is now one of my favorite games!

IF YOU DON'T PLAY, YOU CAN'T WIN

Students of all ages often need a bit (sometimes more than a bit) of external help to get and keep moving. Once they are moving, you'll find it much easier to get them into the game of learning.

Think of playing tennis. Lazy Bess lounging on the grass may not feel very much like whacking a tennis ball around. But if you get her moving around on the court, nine times out of ten she will enter into the spirit of the game—provided she is not discouraged by ridicule or play too difficult for her.

Just as a girl who really knows how to play tennis won't give up on the game because the grass playing surface is too muddy one day, so a student who knows and loves the game of learning can make allowances for interference beyond his control. Bad teachers, foolish assignments, and so on are much more likely to bounce off a child who has been schoolproofed by previous pleasant experiences with the learning game. Such a child will continue to learn *in spite of* the obstacles placed in his way. As a bonus, he will know the problem is the teacher or the assignments, not him.

We can't push this too far, of course. Despite my passionate love of math, two years of an ignorant math teacher in high school almost cured me of math forever. The only way out was to get out of high school early or start learning math on my own. I ended up doing both, thus getting back into the *real* game. This would not have been possible had I not learned that self-study was within the rules of the game, and that the real goal was to get an education, not to attend another year of high school.

Our job, for the rest of this book, is to clarify the rules of the game of learning. Perhaps we can even come up with some improvements over the way the game is currently played! When we know the rules, we will be in much better shape to make sure our children are really playing the game . . . and loving it!

CHAPTER THREE

GETTING UP TO SPEED

B urnout. Home schoolers are burning out. Teachers are burning out. Parents are burning out. Kids are burning out. Consider: how often have you heard anyone say things like:

"I just LOVE school!"
"I adore having my children home with me all day."
"We're expecting our seventh baby. Isn't that great!"
"Oh goody, here come my new eighth-graders."

Now, why do people burn out?

Usually because we are trying to do the wrong thing, or doing the right thing in the wrong way.

Some try to solve motherhood burnout by not having babies, or dumping them all day with others. Similarly, some try to solve educational burnout by sending their home schooled kids off to public school, or by quitting the teaching profession, or (if they are children) by playing hooky. But motherhood and education are not the problem. Ignorant motherhood and bad education are the problems. And the root of both is usually false expectations.

Parents, faced with the demands and diapers of two under-threes, despair and get sterilized because they can't face the thought of that much noise and mess multiplied by two or more. They are forgetting that *kids grow up.* Puff the Magic Dragon lived forever just the same as he always was . . . but "not so little boys." If the little boys are still wearing diapers at age ten, most likely someone forgot their toilet training. If the little girls are still screaming and hitting and throwing things around at age ten, most likely someone forgot their moral and spiritual training. The problem is not with the children, but with the parents' low expectations of what they should require from the children.

The mother of three children under age eight becomes worried about the future of her home school because she is expecting the future to be like the present. Just as much noise. Just as many discipline problems. Just as much confusion on her part about how to teach. "If I'm having this much trouble *now,* how will I ever manage when the baby comes?" she frets. She is forgetting that she is changing and growing and her children are changing and growing. The six-year-old *will* learn to read . . . and then will be able to amuse herself with a book. The eight-year-old *will* learn to multiply . . . and can also learn to help with the baby. The two-year-old *will* learn his colors and shapes . . . and can also learn how to stop ruining the older ones' games. The mother *will* become confident in her teaching . . . if she can only hang on long enough to see some fruit from her work.

If, as we have seen, half of the problem with education today is that we have forgotten students are human, the other half is that *we have forgotten what humans can do.* Human beings are alive. They grow. They even grow up! We should not expect the eighteen-year-old, or even the twelve-year-old, to require as much instruction and discipline as the six-year-old.

In this chapter I want to encourage you to see that education is not all an uphill struggle. Learning and teaching become progressively easier as the learner becomes more disciplined and enjoys it more.

Now, let's look at what you have a right to expect as your children go through the stages of learning, and what you can do to help them through these stages.

THE INPUT STAGES OF TEACHING

The "input" stages are what drive inexperienced mothers to despair and inexperienced teachers to gnash their teeth in frustration. You start out by playing the part of a mama panda bear— carrying your baby with you everywhere. Educationally, this means that, if you want your little one to learn a specific skill, *you* have to supply all the input. *You* have to show Janie how to hold the pencil. *You* have to explain that "we don't color anywhere except on special pieces of paper Mommy gives you." *You* teach the Bible verses, the patty-caking, the toothbrushing. *You* do the diapering and pick up the messes.

Not only do you have to teach your little one, but you have to *re*-teach . . . and reteach, and reteach. You have to supervise while Jimmy picks up his clothes, or at least check up on him frequently. You have to patiently explain for the tenth time that the flash card is an A, not a B. You have to count up to ten hundreds of times, and sing dozens of choruses of the Alphabet Song.

Even as you are working so hard, though, your child is learning much that you *don't* teach him. He is learning to talk, without formal lessons in talking. He is learning to walk. If he is blessed with well-trained older brothers and sisters, he is learning to pick up his messes and play nicely just by following their example. If he is older, he is probably making great efforts to learn how to play games and sports, and to be good at them, too. His greatest lesson, though, is one you much teach him yourself

Learning to Obey

I have a strong distrust of Experts and all their theories. I have an equally strong faith in the Bible's wisdom. This is only reasonable. After all, the Bible claims to be the one and only Word of God. Dr. Infallible, on the other hand, tends to claim divine authority without any vestige of divine inspiration.

Parents, and mothers especially, have carefully followed the dictates of hordes of Doctor Infallibles for the past forty years (longer, if the parents were rich and fashionable). The results have not been encouraging.

Could it be that our overdependence on earthly authorities who come, as the Bible says, "in their own names," is the major reason why parents no longer even dare to hope for respect and affection from their growing children?

Let's forget the Doctor Infallibles for a bit and see what we can learn from the ancient Book of wisdom that has stood the test of thousands of years.

In both Psalms and Proverbs we read that the fear of the Lord is the beginning of wisdom and of knowledge. So how does a child reach the point of fearing the Lord? By the father's discipline, which teaches him to fear his father . . . If some prefer to use the word *respect,* it still comes out the same. Children who are disciplined learn respect for their parents and teachers. And that respect can be transferred to God.

Bruno Bettelheim, a child psychiatrist, has written about fear and learning. Though he cautioned against a crippling fear, he wrote that "while conscience originates in fear, any learning that is not immediately enjoyable depends on the prior formation of a conscience." Thus there

> may be a little learning by the "pleasure principle," but that doesn't go
> very far. For any significant learning, a person must operate by the
> "reality principle" in which rewards are delayed . . . [Bettelheim] does not
> advocate basing academic learning on fear directly. "But the child must
> fear something if he is to apply himself to the arduous task of learning.
> My contention is that for education to proceed, children must have
> learned to fear something before they come to school."
>
> Christian teaching, which includes hell as well as heaven, and which
> includes an all-powerful God continues to instill the old-fashioned fears.
> A large part of the superiority of a good Christian school stems from this.
> Children in such a school come mostly from homes where the fear [or
> respect] or God has been instilled in them. So they bring to school an
> ability to apply themselves to the work of learning . . .
>
> When parents have done their chastening-teaching job well,
> teachers find that children are already motivated to learn. They simply
> step into the parent's place and continue the teaching process.[1]

In the very first Input stage, your little one needs to learn
to obey. As Ruth Beechick just reminded us, "the fear of the
Lord" is the beginning of both wisdom *and* knowledge.
Concentrating your efforts on (1) making sure your child
understands and is capable of following your instructions and
(2) not giving commands unless you intend to back them up,
will save years of grief later on.

Learning to obey is the foundation of all real learning that
comes later. If your student refuses to obey your reasonable
instructions, no amount of gimmicks and bribes will help you
move him one inch.

Of course, you will limit your commands to what your child
can reasonably be responsible for. "Please go sit on the couch,
Marti, and look quietly at a book while I make this telephone
call." "Put away your pencils, Sam, before you get out another
toy to play with." The more specific the command, the better.

Ditto for rules, which are generalized commands: "You may not hit your brother. If he does something wrong, you come and tell me. If for some reason you can't come, yell and I'll come." "You may not throw anything in the house except your Nerf ball." "Be gentle with your books, or we will have to take the books away until you learn to treat them better."

Scripturally, when a child refuses to obey, he should be spanked. He should be made to acknowledge what he did wrong, and after the spanking pray for forgiveness and get a hug. If he continues to rebel, you continue to spank. I should mention, also, that a real spanking is meant to sting without harming. A couple of ineffectual swats on a clothed bottom will only make a child angry. Using what the Bible calls a "rod"—a light, supple object such as those plastic serving spoons sold in your neighborhood supermarket—both eliminates the need for parents whaling away in order to get an effect, and insures the spankee can't get hurt.

Some books I read on child training when I was a new Christian made it sound like spanking magically turned disobedient children into darling angels overnight. In some rare cases, it can have that effect. But most often, the real effect of spanking is to take the tension out of the parent-child relationship. Kids know who is boss. They learn kinesthetically—through their very skin—to respect you. Provided, of course, that you don't frustrate them with unreasonable commands and punishments.

Not every infraction of every rule calls for a spanking. Stealing or destruction of property calls for restitution. Improper treatment of personal possessions results in the possessions disappearing for a time until the child learns to respect them. Laziness in doing a chore may call for Dad walking the child through the chore three or four times. In our family, we call this "practicing." If one of our boys doesn't come quickly when we call him, we tell him to go to the place where he was and call him again. He practices this three or four times, usually giggling the whole time. Extreme laziness to the point of rebelliousness does require a spanking, and might require practicing as well. Willful destruction of property, where the property's value makes restitution impossible, and willful assault both are spankable offenses. So is lying, which gets the most severe penalty of all. We deduct spanks for truth-telling, i.e., "Yes, Father, I cannot tell a lie; I did chop down the cherry tree."

It is your and my responsibility to make sure our children's yokes are easy and their burden is light. Kids have a right to their own opinions, likes, and dislikes, as well as to free time. If Brenda seems at loose ends, give her a choice of edifying things to do: coloring or playing with Legos or reading to little sister, perhaps. Otherwise, Brenda deserves her chance to practice responsibility.

Let me just mention here, in passing, that obedience does not mean you exert your desires and needs at the expense of your children's desires and needs. Thomas Gordon, author of the Parent Effectiveness Training program which in one form or another is being pushed in schools and social service departments as the One Right Way of child-training, assumes as the foundation of his very popular system that children and adults are just two classes fighting over the same territory. He uses only examples that seem to fit his theory, like Dad wanting to sleep and Daughter wanting to play her guitar. But this Marxist view of parent-child relations is completely off-base. Dad does want Daughter to learn respect for others, so she will not get to play the guitar during other people's naps; but Dad will not bang his hammer during her nap, either. The point is that Dad is training Daughter in respect for others, not just trying to survive and get a nap.

We parents want our children to do lots of things that bring us no personal benefit at all. What do you or I gain by insisting that Junior not bash Sally, or that Sam fess up and pay for the neighbors' broken window? I would rather read in my chair than have to get up and spank someone for pinching someone else— and lots of parents do allow this kind of tyranny among their children just because it does not meet their (the parents') needs to have to take the effort to change things. The point is that we are training our children to obey the Higher Law that we also obey. We want our children to treat others respectfully, respect property, and tell the truth for the same reasons that *we* don't insult people on the street, throw rocks through windows, or cheat on our income taxes. We do it because it is *right*. Our children should do it because it is *right*. They should obey us, and we should strive to be worthy of their obedience, because it is *right*.

Learning to Follow Oral Instructions

Learning to follow instructions is a different thing altogether from learning to obey. Now you are trying to teach your little one how to concentrate, remember, and perform particular skills.

At first, a child will be able to remember only one simple instruction, like "Please pick up that paper." At this stage, he can easily be distracted on the way to performing even that simple a task. This is not disobedience, but immaturity. As time goes on, and your youngster gets in the habit of obeying your simple orders cheerfully, you will find that he can remember more complicated instructions. "Go into the living room and bring me the purple book on the couch." Finally, he will be able to perform quite complicated tasks. "Go into the living room and find the purple book that Suzy put somewhere— I don't know exactly where. Inside it is a piece of paper I'd like to show you. Bring it back here, and if you can remember, please pick up a pencil and bring that too."

Learning to follow oral instructions like these is essential practice for learning. It is basic to all cultures. In fact, some of the most successful new foreign language programs for young children start out right here, with the children following instructions given in the foreign language like "Touch your head. Jump. Pick up the pencil."

You are still *giving* the instructions, of course, and you still have to supervise the results. This means you have to be right on hand, and although you are making important progress you may feel somewhat discouraged. *But,* you are about to emerge into the next step.

Learning to Follow Written Instructions

Here you get your first glimmer of hope. Once Junior has learned to read, you need not stand at his shoulder telling him everything he should do in his studies. The workbook page may very well have all the needed instructions right on it. Now it's time for a cup of tea, while Junior takes charge of his own education, right?

Well, not quite right yet. Learning to follow written instructions requires not only clear written instructions and good reading skills, but a certain amount of self-motivation. Little children tend to get discouraged when nobody checks on their progress, and they like to ask questions. At first you should count on explaining the written instructions, or at least reading them aloud with your child and answering his questions. But take heart: you are getting close to a major breakthrough!

THE MOMENTUM STAGES OF TEACHING

I call these the Momentum Stages because, at long last, your learner will be moving on his own steam. He will be seeking out learning on his own, and doing more than you expect. It's a little bit ike jump-starting a car on level ground. At first you have to push. You sweat and strain. You get weary. You may feel like giving up. But after a bit, the car starts to pick up momentum and move on its own. Throw out the clutch, and the engine kicks in and the car moves off under its own power.

Children are not cars, but they are born with "engines": that innate ability to grow and move on their own. At first the engine is practically useless as far as moving the child towards obtaining his own academic education. It lacks "fuel," that is, skills and data. As you train your learner to obey and follow instructions, and give him the basic tools of learning, he gradually can and should take over, until he is driving himself. Your position then becomes that of a guide more than that of a teacher. You can sit back and admire while he learns without any serious effort on your part.

Following Written Instructions on His Own

After following written instructions with your close supervision, the student is ready to move to following written instructions on his own. He will still want to show you what he has accomplished, of course, and you will need to give him helpful feedback and explain any sticky spots. Still, you have gained a lot. During a one-hour math lesson, you may actually need to spend only five minutes helping your learner, whereas at the beginning you had to be there helping for the entire hour.

Making up His Own Course of Study with Help

Now come the first real steps of independence. Your learner now is ready to make up his own course of study with your help and only infrequent supervision. This is what colleges call "independent study." You act as a resource person, helping him find new sources of information and perhaps brainstorming projects, but your formerly little one has now moved beyond the basics and is starting to develop his own tastes and direction. This stage, so beloved of writers of home schooling books, can actually occur at an extremely young age. A five-year-old can become immensely interested in butterflies, or a three-year-old in learning to paint. In these particular areas, even a little child who has learned good concentration can do amazing things on his or her own. That does not mean he can't be at quite an early stage in other areas— for example, reading or cooking. But every bit of worthwhile independence, if nurtured, will spill over into increasing responsibility in other areas. This includes being willing to put aside the beloved task to attend to one less delightful— a valuable lesson for us all to learn!

Inventing and Following
His Own Independent Course of Study

Finally, complete maturity means that the learner is capable of developing his own plan of study and following it through with no oversight by anyone. Many of us have not yet arrived at this stage, since it was never a part of our training. We sign up for a course when we know we could have learned the material from the book, just because we feel the need of some accountability to force us to study. Still, this step should be there before us, as a goal. The person who has reached this step counts, by society's standards, as a bit of a genius, and is well on his way to accomplishing something significant in life.

So now you can see why the mother of three does not really need to worry. Our children can learn to do anything we can do, as long as we are willing to believe in them and discipline them. They are made in the image of God; fallen, yes, but not destroyed. You *can* get back more than you put in. What a beautiful gift from God!

PART II

SIMPLE
IS
BEAUTIFUL

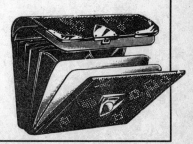

CHAPTER FOUR

A PLACE FOR EVERYTHING

Teacher: "Why haven't you started your math,
Johnny?"
Johnny: "My book is lost."

A journey of a thousand miles really does start with a single step. And frequently travelers miss their journey entirely by forgetting to pack some essential. So let's begin at the beginning: the materials we use to teach with. We're not talking about primers and math texts, but pencils, pens, art supplies, and chalkboards. Once we get these under control, we will have more energy for the creative matter of teaching.

Please don't think I'm being trivial by starting my simplification efforts with the little matter of how we handle our school supplies. More lessons are derailed due to lost pencils, missing chalk, vanished maps, and books that are "around here somewhere— but *where?*" than all other causes combined, including California earthquakes and Maine snowstorms. If you've been teaching for any amount of time, whether at home or otherwise, you know what I mean. The pencil that breaks just before the test (and no other pencil can be found in a ten-mile radius); the missing lesson book that the whole family spends half an hour looking for; these are the killjoys of education. If you don't have the tools with which to write, you can't practice writing. If you can't find the atlas, you can't find the map. If you can't find the map, you can't find Pompeii on the map, and another lesson on geography and Roman history bites the dust.

So, to make all our lives easier, we can start by making the tools of study available. "A place for everything and everything in its place" prevents clutter and mess, and means we don't have to worry about anything but teaching. Which, as many people have noted, is worry enough.

PLAYING STORE

First, a little word on a subject dear to my heart: storage. I hope this section doesn't apply to you. I hope you are not one of those people who feel guilty about "wasting" money on places to put things. I hope you don't store excess clothes in old supermarket brown bags, or leave books in piles on the counter because you lack bookcases. It would make me feel much better if your cleaning supplies are not jammed into a closet from whence they all fall on your head every time you pull out the mop.

I hope you don't suffer from any of the above, because I suffered from it for so long myself. I was firmly convinced that anything expensive floor-to-ceiling bookcases could do, concrete blocks and old boards could do better. (Except be stacked more than three high, because then they topple over and break your foot.) "File drawers?" I would laugh incredulously. "Why waste money on those when we have all these lovely free cardboard boxes of different shapes and sizes with which to decorate our living space?" Pencils and pens were left just anywhere, and in consequence I could never find a pencil or a pen. Books could be buried in any of the dozens of piles on the floor—or, when we graduated to cinder blocks and boards, stuffed haphazardly on any particular shelf in any particular room. And don't let's even talk about how I stored my cleaning supplies, except to note that I had a good reason for only mopping the kitchen floor once every two months.

Every week for years and years I spent several hours of precious time looking for things because I thought that storage was a waste of money. After all, we could buy more *things* with the money I saved on not getting storage; yet more and more things that I would never, ever find when I needed them . . .

Since I was the only one inconvenienced, and we really didn't own that much anyway, I was able to put up with this sad state of affairs for quite a while. But then we had children. Hundreds of little socks and diapers and shoes and bubble suits. Dozens of little read-to-me books. Millions of detachable pieces from only ten or so toys (funny how they multiply). Still I hung in there, searching for the matching sock and disappearing toy pieces. It wasn't until we started home schooling that I began to see I couldn't keep this up.

"Get your pencil and your book and come sit next to Mommy. We're going to learn some fun things about letters today."

(Five minute delay) "Mommy, I can't find my pencil!"

"Look in my drawer."

"There's nothing there but a couple of pencil stubs with the erasers chewed off."

"Well, try the kitchen counter."

"Nope, none there either."

(I join the search, finally unearthing a usable pencil under a couch cushion.)

"All right, here's a pencil. Now come and we'll start."

"Mommy, I can't find my book. . ."

A barrel of laughs, right? Picture this multiplied by three or four children, who can't find any book for any subject because they never were given a particular place to put their books, and the baby so loves to toddle around with books . . .

I would now like to publicly thank Don Aslett, "America's Number One Cleaning Expert," in honor of whose book *Clutter's Last Stand* one of the chapters in *this* book is named, for bringing me to my senses. After being taught for years that a good wife never throws anything out (it might be useful some day, you know!), I finally found out that time is worth more than junk, and the less junk you have the less you have to organize, and that you *should* organize your things if you hope to ever use them, and that if you don't expect to ever use them you should pitch them. Revelation! Don's books apply to cleaning house, but I rapidly found that his principles apply to organizing school supplies as well. Hence, my one contribution to Home Organization Theory:

> Pride's Rule: *If it's not worth finding a special place for, throw it out. You'll never find it anyway.*

Now that you've thrown out all that useless stuff (old mimeos, ballpoint pens that don't write and never did, activity kits based on the visit of Halley's comet, workbooks your child half-finished before you agreed that they were too boring to inflict on an intelligent human), let's get the rest organized!

UP AGAINST THE WALL

You bought that time line. Or Suzy made it. It's a wonderful time line. So educational! So loaded with important historical and cultural information! But it's still sitting in the tube it came in . . . or buried in a pile of educational material . . . or stuffed in the back of a closet.

Bite the bullet. Get out your stapler and tack it up on the wall. Sure, the staples will make little holes. They always do. But why did you buy the time line if you never were going to put it up on the wall? Or why did Suzy have to spend forty hours on something so educational she will never see again? And don't try to say you intend to put it up some day with Scotch tape, so as not to mar the wall. You know, and I know, that Scotch tape (and even worse, magic removable tape) can't hold anything bigger than a postcard on a wall for longer than a week. Not if anyone ever breathes heavily in that room, or if the window is ever opened.

Now, those adorable bulletin boards. I am really sorry that someone made you put those in your school . . . or that you got one for your house. Now you will have to spend the rest of your life collecting bulletin board sets and hand-crafting bulletin board brighteners, none of which will be worth a nickel the day you take it off. There are a few exceptions, but by and large commercial bulletin board stick-ups give precious little information in a precious huge format. And I've never seen a child who thought the world would end if Thanksgiving rolled around and he didn't get to put a construction-paper feather with his name on it on the Thanksgiving bulletin-board turkey. (None of this applies, of course, if you enjoy bulletin boards as art for art's sake.)

Posters, on the other hand, for those unafraid of staple holes, are as good as wallpaper for decorating a kid's room, generally have a lot more info per square inch, and cost a bunch less. They also tend to cost less than the more-sturdy bulletin board sets, so you can throw them anyway someday without tears and regrets. One problem: posters designed for schools, again, tend to spread out and eat the wall. This is so the nearsighted children in the back of the classroom have something edifying to look at while they are ignoring the teacher and her carefully-prepared lesson.

Maps also, naturally, belong on the wall. Anything that takes you time to dig out and keeps rolling up while you try to look at it will never get looked at more than once. If you don't want to cover precious wall space with a map or maps, an atlas works well. If you just adore maps, you can buy one of those gizmos schoolteachers use that has lots of maps rolled up like window shades. You just pull down the one you want. But no fair sticking this marvelous invention in the closet! If you can't bear to have it out where you can see it, you are unlikely to haul it out often enough to justify spending the money on it.

In general, anything you want people to look at and browse goes well on a wall. Providing, of course, you are not one of the kind of people who decorate your home with an eye to potential visits from *House Beautiful* magazine. And walls include mirrors (Bible verses stuck up on Post-its) and windows. But save yourself some trouble: don't bother putting anything educational up on your wall that can be mastered in a short period of time. Handwriting alphabet strips, alphabet and number charts, a Books of the Bible visual, and similar items with long-term educational value will make you happier with your investment than a four-foot by four-foot full-color poster of Parts of the Mouth.

IN THAT CASE

Forget gold and bonds. Bookcases are the home schooler's Number One investment in worldly happiness. Place enough of them in the areas where people like to relax, make up some simple scheme for what books go where (e.g., library books in the right bookcase, family books in the left, school books on the top left), tell the kids how your scheme works, and worry no more.

A good rule to make: No taking out a new book until you've put the one you were reading back.

Reference works demand special treatment. These go best near where people like to study. And reference books you want to see *used* should be accessible. Lock up the family diamonds if you must (or replace them with zircons and stop worrying about thieves); but don't lock up the encyclopedia or put the dictionary on a five-foot-high shelf unless you really don't want anyone to use them.

Schoolbooks do not go well inside desks. That is why the schooldesks we bought three years ago have taken the Long Hike out of our house. Desks mean books are piled on top of each other in dark spaces where the lid is likely to fall upon your head as you search for a book. And piles are deadly. Books get torn, mislaid, and even lost when they are piled.

Note: The new-type schooldesks don't have lids and book storage spaces—not because disorganized book piles have gone out of style, unfortunately, but because today's kids will steal even schoolbooks if they are left where they can get them. Also, it's harder to hide the snub-nosed revolver with which you intend to blow away your English teacher in a wire rack on the back of your seat.

Back to our subject: items which belong stored in cases. This most emphatically includes video and audio tapes and records. An adequately sized cassette storage rack next to your cassette player, combined with a little simple training about Putting Cassettes Back After You Play Them, will eliminate the agonized headaches over where your *Songbirds of North America* tape disappeared to. (It lay on the counter for a while, then got swept with some other stuff into a kitchen drawer. You found it yesterday, and it had only been missing for two years!) Again, if you have *lots* of cassettes, some simple scheme for keeping your Baroque music collection separate from the foreign language instruction tapes will help a lot. If you have *lots and lots* of cassettes, consider giving some away. You can't possibly spend all day every day listening to them or watching them just so as to work through your collection every so often, and you really shouldn't feel you have to try.

A simple solution to the problem of ten people in a family, each with his or her own cassette player and therefore his or her own pile of cassettes (through which everyone else must plow every time they are looking for a particular tape): less cassette players. One cassette player for family listening and family studies, and another for one person at a time to use for personal listening (after which he returns that cassette to the central storage case), ought to be plenty.

IN SIGHT

You want your little darling to play that expensive musical instrument you bought or rented for her, don't you? Well, in this case, out of sight, out of mind. If the tiny violin is stored away in its tiny case in the top of the closet, you can bet it will only come out once a day, and you will have to initiate every violin session. If you can be brave enough to leave the violin where she can get at it by herself, your daughter may well surprise you by how often and how willingly she practices.

Of course, you will be sensible. You won't leave the violin (or flute, or guitar) lying around for the baby to use for batting practice. But any child old enough to play a musical instrument can reach fairly high, or climb on a piano bench to retrieve something from on top of the piano.

The same goes for educational equipment you want people to be able to use on their own, like globes. Your average globe is not such a frail object that it will shatter if placed where the younger family members can reach it. In fact, we sometimes let our baby play with our globe to cheer him up. Perhaps this doesn't apply to those who own $200, light-up-in-the-dark models with oaken floor stands. But your basic $10-$20 globe that kids can handle may prove to be a better investment than the fancy-Dan version that they never get near.

OUT OF SIGHT

Some educational materials do belong out of sight. Gooey stuff. Messy stuff. Breakable stuff. If you would panic when told that your toddler is getting into it, put it up high where he can't.

Many art supplies belong in this catalog. Crayons, for example. It's funny about crayons; some kids will color and neatly put them away, others will break them and try to eat the fragments. Some kids will draw nicely on the paper; others will try to draw nicely on your walls. We have a crayon-eater-and-graffiti-artist, so all the crayon boxes are up good and high.

Paints, gooey pastes, glitter, colored sand, and anything else you don't really want to see in your rug belong where you can control them. How difficult it should be to access depends on how responsible your children are and how often they use these materials. You don't want to spend the rest of your life locking and unlocking cabinets if you can help it. On the other hand, art supplies are usually the sort of thing that children can be counted on to ask for and wait for, unlike more overtly educational stuff like dictionaries. (We just stick it all on a high shelf that the adults can easily reach.)

Science supplies often do best up, up and away. I'm thinking of microscopes and their accompanying glass slides, and burners, and test tubes, and anything yukky that the baby might eat by mistake, like the frog for Junior's dissecting experiment. If Junior is a responsible older boy, he can have his very own lab with everything all neatly set up. But if he has little brothers and sisters, and no room to which the door can be positively certainly padlocked at all times, dangerous and breakable items belong where the brothers and sisters can't get them.

Ant farms and other "live" experiments full of interesting pests: if I had my druthers, they wouldn't come near the house. The barn is a good place for these, provided the cow doesn't object. Failing that, try a shed. Failing that, try a dark night and a sneak trip to the dumpster.

AT YOUR FINGERTIPS

Pens, pencils, paper, and such ought to be where anyone can find them, except the baby. You can manage this two ways: (1) buy so many writing implements that everyone has a few for his pockets and a dozen remain for the central drawer, or (2) rigorously demand that each of these go back into the central drawer as soon as it is no longer needed. I must confess we use option one, but then, we are all writing something every hour of every day.

We keep our paper supplies in a low cabinet, and our scissors and glue sticks in a desk drawer. Casualties of this approach have been some locks of Magdalene's hair, and her doll's, that I didn't really want to spare. So far, no glue in the rug (I'm grateful!). In our case, our desire to give our children access to these very basic and not overly messy creative tools outweighs our desire to prevent all preventable accidents.

Let me encourage you, if you'd like to *really* get organized, to get a copy of Don Aslett's great book *Clutter's Last Stand* (available at bookstores everywhere). Now, organized and with sharp pencils at the ready, on to the next chapter!

CHAPTER FIVE

TWENTY WAYS TO PRESENT A LESSON

The first time I read a book of teaching ideas, I was *impressed*. The author, with nonchalant ease, whipped off two or three truly clever ideas per page— everything from how to make puppets from brown paper bags to a recipe for homemade play dough. "How did this woman get so creative?" I wondered.

Then I read some more books, including a couple of hundred teacher's manuals. A pattern began to develop. Soon I found I could invent my own ways of teaching any given lesson.

Teachers, I found, are not all marvelously creative people who go around inventing teaching methods from scratch. Rather, good teachers are marvelously creative people who have learned some basic ways to approach any teaching problem. The difference between such a teacher and the average mom or dad is that the teacher has learned to *think like a teacher.* He or she has a framework of approaches into which new ideas easily and painlessly fit. The *really* good teachers also have an instinctive sense as to which approach works best for each situation as it arises.

Now, how can we learn to think like teachers? One obvious way is to find a good teacher and follow her around. But suppose you don't have the time for this? Another way that works is to get hold of some really good teaching material and analyze it. But suppose you don't have the time for this either, or that you are not sure of what is good or bad teaching material and don't want to end up imitating a bad example?

Teachers use only a few basic methods, alone or combined, to present all their lessons. Know these methods and you can get a handle on teaching. Know which method works when, and which deserve to be avoided like the Black Plague, and you will feel like a pro! This does not mean that methods alone can make an excellent classroom teacher out of a neophyte, as the poor harassed classroom teacher has additional little matters to deal with, like controlling thirty students who would rather be playing outside. But when it comes to teaching one-on-one, or dealing with a group of students who actually want to learn, you will know as much as anyone about how to make the lesson fly.

READ TO ME

Simple. Open the book and read. No stress for you or the student. Works for all ages and all subjects. You can even discuss what you're reading as you read it. This method is not used nearly enough.

THE LECTURE

We are all acquainted with this time-honored method. Teacher stands up in front of class or student. Teacher speaks. Student listens. Sometimes student takes notes or asks questions. Other times student falls asleep.

Although lecturing is falling out of favor in our egalitarian society, it is still a very worthwhile way to convey large amounts of information in a relatively short amount of time. When the teacher knows a lot more than is found in the book, it would be a shame to pass up the chance to share that knowledge out of some squeamish fear of appearing too authoritative. When the teacher is only trying to teach out of the book, however, lectures become inexcusably boring.

THE DEMONSTRATION

"Ya wanna see how we put a wheel back on a car? Then watch and shut up. Ya slide the wheel on, like this. Ya tighten up the nuts . . . like so. Do it good and tight. Then ya stick on the hubcap. Nuthin' to it." A method that works well with kinesthetic (hands-on)-type people and kinesthetic tasks: knitting, painting, handwriting, cooking. Not good for most social studies work. Impossible for nuclear physics.

THE VISUAL

Teacher-Made Visuals

You sketch rapidly on the blackboard. "This is what a human heart looks like. Here is the aorta. See how the blood flows down, through, and out the other side of the heart?" A few deft chalk strokes can unveil hidden mysteries.

Drawing is truly an excellent method for showing how things work, or what they look like. It's a pity they never taught us how to draw in school . . . (For resources that will teach you to draw, at least well enough to present interesting lessons, see *The Next Book of Home Learning*.)

Canned Visuals

You point to the colorful picture held in your hand or pinned to the wall. "Look at the darling little ducky, children. (Stop squirming, Alicia.) See his bright little yellow bill and his little webbed feet. See his downy little feathers and his stubby little tail." Kids can only stand to look at pictures for so long. Lectures-plus-pictures, as in the example just given, tend to be trite or distracting or both.

One excellent use of pictures is in the study of art. The schools Charlotte Mason founded made extensive use of small art reproductions, which the children kept and handled themselves. Today Calvert School, a major correspondence program, continues this tradition. My *Next Book of Home Learning* lists quite a few new resources for people who want to get acquainted with art this way.

Complicated processes (such as steel forging) and complicated items (such as human anatomy) become much clearer when spelled out visually. Also, practice in becoming observant is useful in itself. Thus it may be better to let students look than to tell them what they are seeing, at least until they ask.

Benefits of Unfolding Visuals

Professional presenters know that multi-layer visuals hold interest much better and are better teaching devices than simple visuals. For instance, in our example above of the teacher drawing a heart, there is "action" in this picture: the action of the teacher drawing each new part. Canned visuals can also have "action." Transparent overlays placed on one by one focus attention— and keep it focused— better than one transparency with reams of information on it. Any picture to which you add pieces as you talk— as in the classic flannelgraph lesson— holds attention better than a picture with all pieces originally in place. Provided, that is, that the audience can't predict what will come next.

THE IMAGINATIVE PICTURE

"The gloomy old castle rose up in the mist behind the moat. Its walls of massive gray stones, broken only by a few small, high, barred windows, frowned down on the weary travelers. Raised up on its iron chain, the stout oaken drawbridge wedged tight against the castle wall presented the very opposite of an hospitable welcome." Good for helping students see with their mind's eye what you have neither the skill nor the time to draw, nor the visual aids to present. The more detailed and emotional the mental picture, the more memorable. E.g., a detailed story about castles will help the hearers remember much more about castles than a dry lecture.

When our second son was having trouble forming some of his letters, we would use imagination to help him visualize the letters. "Little B has a big belly" (emphasizing the B sounds). If he wrote his letters crookedly, we might say something like, "Oh, dear! That poor F must have been hit with a car! See, he's leaning way over instead of standing up straight. Can you help him stand up straight?" Joe would giggle and fix the F without getting upset about his initial mistake. Soon we found him correcting his handwriting on his own, talking to himself about "this poor little squashed O" and so on. Today, by the way, he has excellent handwriting.

A note of warning here: the coercive use of imagination, ordering children to imagine spiritual scenes having nothing to do with any valid educational purpose, is gaining in favor in educational circles. This is a pagan religious practice, nothing more or less. It certainly does make students more susceptible to lesson material— and to worse things as well. Inviting "imaginary" spirit guides into your head is not something to play with.

Imaginative pictures, however, need not imply occult content. Jesus Christ presented imaginative pictures (e.g., His parables).

THE MOVING PICTURE

Turn off the lights. Turn on the TV or film projector or video player. The kids watch the lesson. This is a way to present information, all right, even if it isn't teaching. More about this teacher-saving (but often misused) presentation method in Chapter 7.

THE EXPERIENCE

"Put a seashell to your ear and 'listen to the sea.' What you really hear is your own blood rushing by your inner ear!" This is an actual "experience" presentation taken straight from the KONOS curriculum.[1]

You, the teacher, collect materials necessary to The Experience. You then let the child experience them. However, as in the example just given, it helps a lot if you give the child a clue or two as to what he just experienced.

Experiences are necessary to the study of science, considerably less so for other subjects. They are almost always fun, though, and consequently popular with students and with teachers who are tired of the classroom routine.

THE EXPERIMENT

"Collect some glass jars of the same size. Pour different amounts of water into each. Now, tap each jar with a spoon.

Note which jar makes the highest tone and which the lowest."
Here you have an experiment. The difference between an
experiment and an experience is that in an experiment you are
either (1) checking to see if what you were taught works, or
(2) varying inputs to see how they affect results. In this
experiment, you were varying the amount of water in each jar
and observing how this affected the tone the jar made when
struck with a spoon.

Experiments are wonderful for teaching the student to
check out what he is told instead of blindly accepting it. They
are also wonderful for helping students to discover principles
on their own and remember them. Lastly, students can learn
the scientific method through a well-chosen course of
experiments.

Although experiments are most frequently used in science
programs, you can develop experiments for all subjects. Some
examples: "Translate the first paragraph of Dickens' *A Tale of
Two Cities* into modern journalese. Is it more impressive
emotionally or less?" for language arts (studying the effect of
literary styles on audience impact). "Take two cubes. Add
another four cubes to them. How many cubes do you have?"
(math).

Math manipulatives, as in the last example, provide a way
for students to double-check that math works while perhaps
discovering additional math principles on their own. Language
arts experiments are harder to design and therefore not as
common.

Social studies experiments are impractical, impossible, or
unethical. You can't reach back into history and twiddle the
inputs. Neither can the average student put groups of people
through controlled experiments to "see what happens." Some
of us also have serious reservations about accredited
researchers treating humans like guinea pigs for social

experiments. Thus, the next presentation device: the simulation.

THE SIMULATION

Simulations enable your students to try dangerous or inaccessible experiments. Computer simulations of science experiments are one example. So are board games. So are models of items like the human heart or race cars. Your student can play a war game without risking his life (or anyone else's) in war, or dissect a heart without inconveniencing any owner of a heart. He can take apart a car without having to pay $10,000 for the car, or practice CPR lifesaving maneuvers on an unbreakable dummy instead of a breakable classmate.

Science, engineering, and social studies are traditionally prime areas for simulations. Now that computers are available, we have math simulations too. Brøderbund Software's *Geometry* program is an excellent example of a math simulation. The program, a textbook-on-disk, includes "experiments" (really, simulations) like triangles whose angles you can increase or decrease to observe the effect on the other angles.

The human race has managed for thousands of years without simulations. And an inaccurate simulation is worse than no simulation at all. Still, if you can afford the cost in time and dollars, simulations are both fun and memorable.

WALK ME THROUGH IT

"May I hold your hand, Blake? Good. Let's trace the letter A in the air." "Tuck down your head, Fran. Now I flip your seat and legs over . . . like so . . . and you've done your first somersault!" Sometimes kids just don't get it until you physically put them through the steps. Officially this is called "kinesthetic teaching," and for physical activities like handwriting and athletics it's a lot less time-consuming than trying to explain complicated processes in words. For strongly kinesthetic learners, this may be the *only* way you will ever be able to explain desired physical actions.

Closely allied to this is the practice of "patterning," used usually with brain-damaged or handicapped people. When the ear-gate or eye-gate has problems, you can bypass them both by putting information in through the learner's muscles and skin. Clap their hands together to teach them to clap. Move their legs in crawling motions to teach them to crawl. It works.

ASK ME TO LOOK IT UP

"OK, class. You have ten minutes to find out what kind of houses the Cree Indians built and where they lived." "Clark, since we are studying World War I heroes, why don't you get down the encyclopedia and look up Henry Johnson?" You are asking the student to discover his own information instead of feeding it to him. If you have already taught him how to research, you could simply ask him to find out about a subject without telling him where to look. Otherwise, you can teach research skills at the same time as the information being researched by telling him where to find the facts.

Research skills separate the men (people who have learned how to learn) from the boys (people who need to be spoon-fed knowledge). They apply to every subject and can be used in every subject.

CHALLENGE ME

"Adam, you just said you think cats make better pets than dogs. Can you give us some reasons why cats are better pets?"

"Cats are quieter. They don't bark."

"But couldn't barking be useful sometimes? What about watchdogs? Isn't it useful for a dog to bark at intruders?"

"Maybe. But lots of dogs bark all the time, not just at burglars. And barking gets on my nerves. Also, cats are less expensive to feed, and you don't have to walk them."

"You're right about the expense. But is expense, or lack of it, the main reason people choose a pet? Also, some people appreciate the regular exercise they get walking a dog. I know one man whose doctor suggested he buy a dog to walk in order to improve his heart condition."

"If you need the extra exercise, I suppose that's OK. But lots of people are tired after a day's work and don't feel like walking a dog."

Socrates is famous for popularizing this kind of discussion. The teacher questions the student, trying to help him see when his ideas are really logical and realistic and when they are simply emotional opinions. Thus, the student learns logic and argumentation.

WARNING: This method can be used simply to relentlessly challenge legitimate beliefs. A child may believe something true, yet not be able to logically defend it against attack.

ACT IT OUT

Voice Dramatization • Bodily Dramatization
Costumes • Props
Puppets • Ventriloquism • and So On

These headings speak for themselves. First, presenting material using only your own voice and body movements. Examples: reading aloud with expression, sound effects, and accents; demonstrating fencing with an imaginary sword. These methods are economical and freely available, as well as giving you a chance to use that long-neglected dramatic talent! You can also get fancy, coming to class dressed as Lady Liberty, carrying a flaming torch, and armed with an Enrico the Immigrant puppet or ventriloquist dummy. The latter makes a bigger effect— at first, anyway— but is *much* more time-consuming.

Dolls, puppets, and so on are easy for teachers to use. But *why* are you hiding behind that puppet? Entertainment value? Or is there some more sinister reason? Percentage-wise, it seems that puppets are used much more often for teaching character lessons and eternal truths than for math and phonics. Do we adults fear that kids won't listen to us if we just tell them this stuff straightforwardly? Do we think a puppet has more authority with the kids than us? Are these lessons such bitter pills that we need to sweeten them with dramatic staging and adorable mannikins?

FIELD TRIPS

You know all about these. Visit the museum. Go to Sturbridge Village. Tour the local widget factory. Trek the Appalachian Trail. A field trip is a great big Experience that you have to drive to. Gives you lots to talk about afterwards. Takes a lot of time. The more natural the trip site, the more really useful data you bring back on that subject. Historical simulations and museum slide shows are not as authentic as the widget factory, where you actually see real widgets manufactured.

A field trip can either be fun, or it can be a note-taking prelude to a report. Pick one.

REPEAT AFTER ME

"Repeat after me: *Je suis français . . . Tu es français . . . Il est français . . . Elle est française . . .*" "Say what I say: A . . . B . . .

C . . . D . . ." "In the beginning God" (echo: "In the beginning God") "created the heavens and the earth" (echo: "created the heavens and the earth").

Parroting is a perfectly legitimate way to teach memory work, from the Catechism to the alphabet. Repeating aloud cements data in a way that simply reading it or hearing it does not. This is not, however, a good way to teach *understanding*.

SONGS, CHANTS, AND POEMS

"Down and over, down some more: That's the way we make a 4!" "ABCDEFG . . . HIJKLMNOP. QRS, TUV, W, X, Y and Z. Now I know my ABC's. Next time won't you sing with me!" Better than naked parroting. Useful for the same things.

GAMES

Drill and practice time! Boring, boring, boring. Make the drill into a game. Are we copping out here on our responsibility to help the student Learn Like an Adult? No, because drill is ideally suited to games. You can either time the drill (let the student compete against himself, not others, for best results) or make the drill and practice itself into a game. Play 'N Talk's *Spell Lingo* game is an excellent example of this. The child practices new reading techniques with a set of Bingo cards devoted to that skill (e.g., short-vowel words). His slow speed of reading doesn't matter, since Bingo never moves at a blinding rate. He is practicing associating the spoken word with the printed word, but in an enjoyable game-like way.

Some subjects are games in their own right: sports, for example. Others are easily made into games, like math. Yet others are too serious for clowning around. I can't picture making a study of the Holocaust, or of Stalin's deliberate starvation of millions of Ukranians, into a game. (If there is such a game, don't tell me. I don't want to know.)

HERE IT IS, YOU FIGURE IT OUT

You walk up to your learner with an armload of workbooks, library books, hands-on material, whatever. You drop it in front of him. "Here's everything you need to learn about this subject. You figure it out."

As long as you actually give your learner enough information in that armload you dropped on him, you are not necessarily being cruel. If he has the gumption to tackle it and try to learn on his own, he will really understand and remember what he learns.

BAD WAYS TO PRESENT A LESSON

An infinite number of bad lessons lurk out there in the educational wasteland, but only a finite number of bad ways to present a good lesson. Thank goodness!

The first bad way to present a good lesson is to pick the wrong presentation method. Teaching the ABC's with a "Here it is, you figure it out" approach seldom bears immediate good fruit. Asking students to imagine complex geometric relationships in their heads (instead of simply drawing a picture that shows what you're talking about) is cruel and inhuman punishment. Presenting the Crucifixion with cutesy puppets is likewise ungood.

Some presentation methods are more than a bad choice for a particular subject. The following commonly-used presentation methods are altogether wrong. Period.

Role-Playing Evil

"Donna, pretend you are a female junkie desperate for a fix. You've been a teen prostitute for some time now. Davy, you are a fellow walking down the sidewalk. Now, Donna, approach Davy and try to hustle him." Cute, huh? Some sex ed classes in public school have actually gone through this little number, or similar jolly activities.[2] Or, a little closer to home: "Sandy, you and Ellen are friends. Ellen uses drugs. You just found out about it today. She asks you to use drugs with her. Now you and Ellen role-play this situation." An exercise very similar to this appeared in a "Christian" health book I was sent to review.

Generally, the theoretical goal of evil role play is good. "We want to teach children to resist drug pushers and prostitutes." Lovely. Now can we figure out a way to do this without asking them to practice the roles of drug pushers and prostitutes?

Trivial Pursuits

"Hi! I'm Abraham Lincoln. I freed the slaves." A teacher's magazine I subscribe to is loaded with little playlets with lines like that. Typical plot: student is studying school subject. Characters from that subject appear to the student. They introduce themselves with deathless lines like the above. Eventually characters utter fond farewells and disappear.

I've seen this approach used with literature (literary characters like The Three Bears and Alice in Wonderland invite the students to a game show, "Name That Character"), history (we learn that George Washington was the first President and that Lincoln freed the slaves), social studies (Indian cultures), ad nauseam. The problem is not just that the subject is so colossally dumbed-down. We are used to that. What's special about the Trivializing approach is that *the dumb stuff is put in the mouths of important people.*

What picture of Lincoln does a second-grader get from "Hi! I'm Abraham Lincoln. I freed the slaves"? Would Lincoln *ever* have introduced himself like that? Is it true to the character of The Three Bears to have them as game-show guests? Would the Plains Indians want to be immortalized as dummies with nothing better to do than utter clichés to schoolkids?

The deeper, more subtle meaning of trivializing Abraham Lincoln is that kids come to believe that the whole world is anxious to bow to them. In real life, Presidents are hard to approach, and Alice and The Three Bears need to be approached on their own terms. Not so in the happy never-never land of trivial pursuits. There, a child snaps his fingers and important people rush to his side. Mr. Lincoln gets no respect. And people wonder why kids today seem to have no heroes . . .

Trivial Sermons

Christians have a peculiar variation on the Trivializing theme. We drag out our little box— our "lesson of the week." Then we go around trying it on Bible verses until we find one we can chop to fit into the little box, rather like Cinderella's stepsisters chopping off their toes and heels to try on the glass slipper. Susan Schaeffer Macaulay describes the danger:

> I remember the bright brown eyes of another interesting person, at present aged four. A few weeks ago she was in a small group of children listening to a straightforward biblical narration of creation, of the first persons, and of their deliberate choice to disobey God's command. The children had been deeply attentive and interested. Suddenly the brown eyes flashed. "But, Susan, it isn't *true,* is it?"
>
> How amazed and interested she was when I said that it was indeed true! People five times her age have asked the same question. I cannot see any essential difference. In both cases, it is an intelligent, basic question. . . .

When the story was over, the children left, unselfconscious and relaxed. Two weeks later, they retold me the entire story without one word of prompting.

They had been presented with straightforward history. It interested them, just as history interests adults. They had no need for a little twaddle talk at the end, to tell them how or what to think about what they had heard.

Suppose I had been ill-advised enough to say, "Sit still, Jenny, and don't bring up your ideas about truth right now. Today we are supposed to think about families. So we will think about mommies and daddies and that God made them so they would have a family right at the very beginning."

What would I have been doing?[3]

Well, we all know perfectly well— or at least we *should* know— what Susan would have been doing had she ignored that honest question. She would have been teaching her students that the Bible doesn't *really* matter. What matters is the "lesson of the week." And who made up the lesson of the week? Why, the teacher, of course! (Actually, usually some female-headed curriculum committee somewhere made up the lesson, but the kids don't know that.) "So what they want us to learn in church," the kids reason, "is to believe and obey the teacher and never mind what the Bible says." Great lesson.

You remember how, at the beginning of this book, we discovered that behaviorists think kids are machines, and in order to control these little machines they filter all lesson inputs through a controlled teacher, controlled curriculum, and controlled environment. There is *no* difference between this and the common practice of "teaching" the Bible as a series of morals-of-the-week, all determined by the curriculum provider or even the teacher.

Happily, we have dozens of *good* ways to teach everything— even Bible. You can • read it to your students • show them how you live it • obtain illustrations of biblical plants, animals, architecture, and so on • act out various Scripture scenes • make models (the Tabernacle, a house in Palestine) • ask them to look up verses (easy) or find out what the Bible says about a given subject (challenging) • have them repeat memory verses or the books of the Bible • and so on. No need for trivial canned sermonettes when now you can expertly teach like a *real* teacher!

CHAPTER SIX

TWENTY WAYS TO SHOW AND TELL

P eople are always confusing teaching (putting information out where the student can get it) and feedback (finding out what the student knows). As I said in a previous book, "Teaching is *telling or showing people what they don't know.*" Asking students to show and tell you what they already know is feedback, not teaching!

You do have good reasons for wanting to know what your learner knows. For one thing, you can keep from wasting your time and his. I say this as a student who struggled through her entire academic career with schools that insisted I take courses on material I had already learned on my own! The excitement just leaks out of teaching and learning when the student already understands what you are trying to teach.

Another good reason for finding out what your learner knows is to locate gaps in his knowledge and understanding. Like little cracks in a house foundation, these are best found and mended before you build any further on them.

Finally, as many others have observed, showing what you know tends to reinforce your knowledge. The simple act of explaining or demonstrating knowledge to another cements it in your own mind. In this last sense, getting feedback from your learner tops off your teaching effort.

Here are twenty good and not-so-good ways for your students to show and tell you what they know.

WAIT!

The simplest feedback method of all. Wait until the student voluntarily asks you a question or otherwise shows his new knowledge. You then answer his questions, ooh and aah over his drawing or story, listen to his lecture (kids love to teach the teacher!), and go from there.

This, of course, is the highest-quality feedback of all. Whatever the student brings to you is *his*. He also reveals his interest, or lack of it, without any need for prying.

Why is this method so underused? In the classroom, because teaching deadlines buzz the teacher along like a machine intent on finishing the job on time. In the home, lack of motherly patience is the culprit.

If we believe in treating students like human beings, waiting and giving them a chance to tell us what they know, or don't know, is a fine place to start.

THE OPEN-ENDED QUESTION

"Well, Frank, what do you think?" That is about as open-ended as a question can get. You close the book, or turn off the tape player, or clean up the experiment, and ask the learner what he thinks of it. You may get more of an answer than you bargained for— "It was really stupid and boring." "The Ghost of Christmas Past was really creepy. Yuk!" "I think that next time we should use a real glass beaker instead of a margarine tub, 'cause my experiment ate out the bottom of the tub."

Essentially you are trying to hurry up the process of waiting for the children to raise their own questions and ideas. The success of this method depends entirely on the friendly cooperation of your students. A kid who resents being manipulated will suspect the open-ended question is a wedge to invade his privacy. You might as well have told him, "You have the right to remain silent. Anything you say can and will be used against you . . . " And, if you are more interested in analyzing a student's personality than finding out what he knows, he will be right.

One of the many benefits of treating students like human beings is that they can trust us. Moral: Resolve now never to use what you know about your learners to trick them into doing what you want.

THE QUIZ OR TEST

Quizzing a kid on what he knows is probably the first thing most of us think of when we want to find out what a child knows. Here we have the most-used feedback method. It also typically involves the least real thinking.

Question-answering can take many forms, and does not necessarily have to involve grading.

Verbal Testing

Verbal quizzing can be quite informal and nonthreatening, or the sort of experience that eats the victim's guts out. It all depends on who the quizzing is in front of and what happens if the quizzee fails. Defending your Ph.D. thesis before a hostile faculty is an example of gut-munching verbal testing. In contrast, a few simple questions designed to find out how well the student understands what he just finished studying generally poses no problem, provided that the worst possible

result for the student is no more than having to "do it over."
This is a very time-effective method as long as you can
maintain a friendly attitude. In other words, avoid saying
things like, "I bet you were daydreaming instead of reading
your assignment. Quick, now . . . who is Pericles? Ha! I
thought you wouldn't know!"

Some people, the competitive type, do get sucked into
playing catch-the-student-not-working, a game in which
students join with enthusiasm (their version is bluff-the-
teacher and play-dumb-when-questioned).

If you find yourself in such a battle of wits, back out.
(You're going to lose, anyway.) Try to approach verbal quizzing
with the attitude of finding out what students know, not
catching them in wrongdoing. If old habits are too ingrained to
make this easy, you might try giving testing a rest altogether
and concentrating on giving your students input and letting
them show you what they know in some of the more active,
fun ways listed elsewhere in this chapter.

Paper Testing

You write down the questions or buy tests from your
curriculum publisher. Your students write down the answers.
This method is best used in large classes, where it takes too
long to verbally quiz each student, and for difficult questions
that require time to answer. Students can be permitted to use
reference material as a source for their answers, or be required
to answer strictly from memory, depending on whether you are
testing for information retention or for ability to use a skill.

Reference material usually, but not always, means the
course textbook. At my alma mater, one professor told the
students they could use any source they could physically carry
in to help them on the test. One enterprising young fellow
carried in a graduate student on his back! He may not have

displayed much knowledge of physics, but he certainly showed a quick mind for legal loopholes!

Computer (Interactive) Testing

Instant feedback! Interest! Those are the high points of computer testing, provided of course that you are using a good program. Kids don't have to wait to find out if their answers are correct. With the best software, if a student misses a problem he is given another chance or two to solve it. If he continues to mess up, the problem is explained to him. He is then given more problems of the same type to work with.

Most educational software is of the test-and-reteach variety. It doesn't really teach anything new so much as test and reinforce previous teaching.

Computer testing is OK in moderation, as part of a balanced program that includes lots of human input. Too much time before an electronic quizmaster makes students strange. Would *you* want to become expert at doing what some machine tells you to do?

REPEAT IT

You've told Maggie to wipe her feet on the mat before she comes in the house. You have told her and told her, at least two dozen times. Still there are muddy footprints on the new rug. A problem of disobedience, right? Well, try this first. "Maggie, please wipe your feet on the mat before coming in. What did I just say?" Maggie now has to either (1) admit she wasn't listening (in which case you tell her to listen carefully as you say it again) or (2) admit she was listening. "Fine. Now repeat what I just said again. Good. Say it again." Run through this a few more times and Maggie will have to admit she *knows* she is supposed to wipe her feet on the mat.

A hint: in really tough cases you might also have to walk Maggie through the foot-wiping procedure. She might not know what you mean by "wiping your feet on the mat." Once you have walked her through this a few times, and asked her to repeat the action on her own a few times, you will both know that Maggie knows this rule.

This same procedure applies to any area where you are having difficulty finding out what the student knows. Once he repeats your words or actions several times, he can be held accountable for that knowledge. You both know he knows.

Disciplinary accountability is not the only reason for asking students to repeat your words or actions. Parroting is a teaching device as well, as we noted in the previous chapter. It just happens to be a teaching device with instant feedback built in. And it often is good to find out if your learner remembers exactly what you told or showed him before asking him to do anything complicated with that information.

Areas where student echoing works particularly well: art, music, physical actions, family rules.

SUMMARIZE IT

Summarizing is a step beyond straight repetition, but there is no hard-and-fast line between the two. To summarize an involved explanation requires that the student (1) understand the original teaching, and (2) separate the essential from the extras. This technique provides excellent training in thinking. It is essential for every intellectual profession, from law to engineering.

Charlotte Mason recommended this method exclusively in the early grades, as the children's only required feedback device to let the teacher know what they learned from the books they read or that were read to them.

WRITE IT OUT

Another time-tested method is asking your learner to write an essay, book report, or other summary of what was learned. This requires more effort than narration or verbal summary, and should therefore be used more sparingly.

At the private school I attended for a few years, students were asked each day to write a "Dictée." The teacher would read a literature selection *slowly* and we would try to write it quickly and neatly in our copy books. This was an exercise in memory, spelling, grammar, and handwriting all rolled into one. Given good literature selections, it could be an introduction to fine sentence structure and vocabulary as well.

An alternative is to simply copy material you are trying to learn. Many of us write out Bible verses for this reason. The kings of Israel were each required to write out their own copy of the Scriptures (although few of them seem to have done it).

A written copy of the student's work gives teachers a marvelous sense of security, and is useful for waving in the faces of state education personnel, if you happen to be a home schooler. We all believe what we see, and if your student never produces any written work most people find it hard to believe he knows anything. Keep this in mind.

DISCUSS IT

Discussing is a step beyond summarizing. You turn over the material studied and try to draw conclusions, while other people challenge or buttress your reasoning.

One teacher and one student can have good discussions. Two friends have better discussions.

I would like to suggest that you try entering as an equal (not a moderator or Fountain of Wisdom) into discussions of material learned. Don't be afraid to give your mature, adult opinion even to a two-year-old, or to listen seriously to what she says. "As iron sharpens iron, so one man sharpens another" (Proverbs 27:17).

This doesn't mean you have to treat hare-brained notions and ignorance with kid gloves. "He who walks with the wise becomes wise," but not if the wise are afraid to share their wisdom!

Just as you will never improve as a tennis player by only playing with people who are on your level or worse, your students will never improve their thinking and reasoning if they are condemned to discussions dumbed down to an "age-appropriate level." Give them a chance.

ANALYZE IT

"You know what a kayak is. Now can you tell me why a kayak is well-suited for use in icy rivers?" You will notice that this is really a type of question, rather than a distinctive feedback method. The reason I mention it is that human thinking does not end with repetition and summary. You want to know if your learner truly grasps the subject.

Note that his answer may not be the "right" one in the book. The book may expect him to say, "Because when it turns over in the water the person in it doesn't get dumped out." He might actually say, "Because it is made of materials found in that cold region," or "Because it handles well in swift water," or even, "Because it is small enough to fit in a river." These are not stupid answers. In each case, the student has thought about what makes a kayak a kayak (its materials and shape).

Another possible answer is, "I couldn't care less about kayaks, Mom. After all, we live in Hawaii!" Here the student has analyzed the *question*. Don't jump to the conclusion that he is merely being rude. (That was a rude way to say it, of course, perhaps fueled by frustration.) Kids will analyze all your teaching as well as what you teach. Be open enough to let them point out twaddle and time-wasting clutter, even if you disagree with their analysis of what constitutes twaddle and clutter. You can always explain why it is important for Hawaiians to know about kayaks . . . if it is. Otherwise, you will have taught him that he is not *really* supposed to think, only to lend you his mind to mold as you will— in other words, that he is not supposed to be human. You also will miss out on the important feedback of what your student really thinks of your teaching and lessons, thus destroying a built-in opportunity to improve both. Better to have a student who sounds off occasionally than one who never thinks at all about what he is learning.

COMPARE IT

"So we've looked at how the colonists lived and how the East Coast Indians lived. Now let's compare them. Which way of life was easier . . . more productive . . . more stable? What were the advantages and disadvantages of colonial homes as compared with Indian homes? Of their food? Clothing? Marriage customs?" Comparing is another type of questioning and a step beyond analyzing. Here you already know about colonists and Indians, but have to show how well you really understand what you know.

A step beyond simple comparisons— where the grounds of comparison is supplied for you— is to develop grounds of comparison. You figure out for yourself what you are contrasting with what. In our example above, the grounds of comparison were ease, productivity, and stability. They could just as easily have been pleasure (which way of life was more fun?), religious (which culture had a true religion?), or freedom (which way of life was more free?).

Reviewers and critics have to develop grounds of comparison for comparing the products they are asked to review. As a customer (I hate the word "consumer"!), you have to decide what features of a product are important to you— worth comparing with others— and which are less so. This is the virtue of "discernment," and it applies to your choice of ideas as well as to your shopping.

Charlotte Mason said, and I agree with her, that "the chief responsibility which rests on [students] as persons is the acceptance or rejection of initial ideas."[1] Our job is not to conceal the choices the world offers, but to show our students *why* certain choices are good or evil and *how* to discern for themselves the good and the bad. When we see them making intelligent comparisons on their own, we can know that they have learned at least this most important lesson.

MODEL IT

Looking for a nice, quiet way your student can show what he knows, one that is fun as well? Try asking him to model it.

What can your student model? David confronting Goliath. The human eye. Parts of a flower. The battle of Gettysburg. Conic sections. The letter A. The world. In short, anything that has a shape. You can use any medium you like: papier maché, cloth, wet sand, dough, popsicle sticks, plasticine, beeswax . . . Clay is particularly useful because you don't have to warm it up in your hands to work it, and you can squish the model and reuse it instead of having to choose between saving it forever (clutter) or throwing it out (agony)!

Modeling is time-consuming, especially at first, when the learner is getting used to the medium. However, it does keep kids happy, and provides wonderful tactile reinforcement for your lessons. Plus, you now have an excuse to play with craft materials.

DRAW IT

If modeling is too much work, or takes up too much room, students can show what they know by drawing the lesson. Make an outline map of the United States and fill in the states. Plot out the Battle of the Bulge. Graph the changes in rabbit population versus the change in the number of foxes. Chart St. Brendan's route to America (some say he discovered it in the sixth century!).

Drawing may be the best or only feedback method for a highly physical child, or one with severe speech problems. Often children who sound like they don't understand your questions at all can show you wonders when asked to draw their answers. This, then, is a good bridge-building device, and can also be useful when you are dealing with visual or visualizable data.

ACT IT OUT

**Verbal Dramatization • Bodily Dramatization
Costumes • Props
Puppets • Ventriloquism • and So On**

In the previous chapter, we looked at how you, the teacher, could present material by acting it out. Now the students get in the act!

You can tell a lot about what students understand by the way they dramatize a subject when given the chance. When your student paddles his imaginary kayak as if it were a rowboat, you know he missed the point of that lesson. If he reads the part of Scrooge in a baby voice, you'll know something is wrong (or, more likely, that he is trying to be funny); when he does Christopher Robin with a British accent you know he knows that the author of *Winnie-the-Pooh* was English.

Costumes, props, and puppets are naturals for dramatizing history or literature. Let the class put on *Macbeth* with puppets and they'll remember it forever. Puppets are readily available, and a great equalizer for kids too shy to perform in public.

Costumes and props take a *long* time to prepare. A few generalized props and costumes, like shapeless robes usable as everything from kingly garments to shepherd's robes, are much more handy than fancy, detailed accessories. Similarly, your basic generic puppet (perhaps with a few felt accessories to personalize his features) is a better investment than overly detailed types. A little imagination goes a long way, and it's free, too.

PRACTICE IT

Not much to say here. You listen to or watch his practice, and you know what he knows. Those dreadful squawking noises from the violin mean Yolanda needs more input about proper bowing technique. That neat column of A's tells you George has mastered the handwriting of letter A. As Henry hits the tennis ball into the net for the fourth time, you observe that he is holding his racquet too loosely, and possibly needs wrist-strengthening exercises.

The point here is that you need to *be there*. Practice with nobody observing is worthless as a feedback technique. Typically the student ends up drilling himself in bad habits (wrong bow position, poor penmanship). You want him to *improve*, not just to practice!

USE IT

We all love projects. Many projects involve simply drawing or modeling (making) something already studied. But *some* projects—big-time projects—ask students to apply their knowledge and construct something new. One example: making kites as part of your study of aerodynamics. Another: developing your own recipe for a new kind of bread, based on the most nutritious ingredients you can find.

Projects are time-consuming and generally messy. Thus, it is important to make sure the effort is worthwhile. Also, since the world is full of projects, why not let your student pick the ones that interest him?

TEACH IT

"I'm so glad you are reading so well, Wintergreen. Now let's see you teach your little sister to read." If he can teach it, he knows it. If he can't teach it, he finds out he doesn't know it as well as he thought he did, or that you have failed to teach him how to teach. Keep an eye on Little Sister during this process to make sure she is enjoying it. A real time-saver for teachers.

PRESENT IT

"Today's the big day, Ermintrude! You get to make your presentation on the History of Doll-making!" Presenting is just teaching a group. Because the group has to assemble for this occasion, it requires more formal teaching skill on the presenter's part than merely teaching one other person.

Suggested victims (um, I meant "audience") to whom to present:

- The teacher. This is not too much fun. All that work just to show you what you just taught me?

- The captive audience (other students or family members). Be kind; laugh at me today and I'll laugh at you tomorrow!

- Outsiders (neighbors, relatives, the mailman . . .)

I'll be honest. We absolutely never use this feedback method in our family. Visions of miserable piano recitals (when I was a child) and hours spent explaining the use of visual aids (now that I'm grown up and short on time) dance through my head every time someone mentions presentations. We will show the kids how to do this . . . sooner or later. But right now we feel no compelling need to show off what our kids know to the entire community. (Of course, if you are well-organized, boast lots of patient friends, and have outgoing kids who are highly motivated by the chance to make a presentation, this is a different story.)

CHALLENGE IT

The kid in the back of the room raises his hand. "Mr. Oglethorpe, you put the comma in the wrong place." Nasty little brat, right? Wrong. If he knows enough to point out inaccuracies in your work or the information you give him, you can know this student *really* knows the subject.

Teachers typically ask such students, sarcastically, "If you know so much, how about teaching the course?" I have always wished that, instead of giving in to sarcasm, someday some teacher would actually let the smart-aleck try teaching. We all might learn something.

BAD WAYS TO SHOW AND TELL

Parroting-Without-Questioning

Parroting-without-questioning means, "Hush up and just repeat what I tell you." This is denying the student's right to challenge and understand. We always have to leave room for the learner to question us. Otherwise it's education for robots, not people.

Prying

"What is your favorite . . . most embarrassing . . . least liked . . . ? Tell us about your moral behavior . . . friendships . . . family problems." This is the Spanish Inquisition, not a legitimate feedback method.

I don't care how much publishers rationalize that children are motivated by babbling about themselves. Aside from being a fine excuse for building totally self-centered character, the sea of prying questions found in so many workbooks and handouts nowadays is nothing more or less than an inexcusable invasion of privacy.

Some teachers have a secret compulsion to unravel their students' insides. You can always spot these folks because they give higher marks for embarrassing self-revelations than for good writing. I blush to admit that in the eighth grade I quite deliberately cranked an A out of one such woman with maudlin stories about how my family didn't understand poor little me. It was what she *wanted* to hear.

Priers are never eager to hear good news. They want to discover your problems so they can pin you on a card. This has nothing whatsoever to do with finding out what students know . . . except that they know how to give the teacher what she wants, even if it is humiliating and stupid.

The Hot Seat

This is actually a behavior modification technique. You humiliate the student by asking him about a subject that he has obviously not prepared. The class then snickers at his ignorance, he wishes he could die, and theoretically resolves never to come to class unprepared again. Actually, he has lost so much face that he probably is resolving simply never to come to class again if he can help it.

The subtler message in this kid-sized version of the Lifeboat Game is that we learn only to please the teacher and our classmates, and that only the strong survive.

HOW TO SCHOOLPROOF AGAINST BAD FEEDBACK METHODS

One of the great benefits of teaching your own children at home is that you can protect them against the humiliation and frustration of bad feedback methods. A mind is a terrible thing to waste, and teaching kids that school is where they go to be humiliated is a great way to waste it.

If your child attends such a school, the best way you can schoolproof him is to *get him out.* Failing that, you can at least explain to him why the feedback methods used on him are wrong and encourage him to quietly resist them.

There is no way to totally schoolproof a five-year-old against questions and feedback techniques designed to destroy his faith in God, trust in you, and hope for the future. Think twice, and more than twice, before sending your child to the public schools, where such techniques have been designed and perfected for the past twenty years.[2] An older child may be able to resist these intrusions, but meanwhile he certainly won't be getting the best education available. You will have to afterschool him on your own time to provide the human education that the behaviorists and humanists don't. It may well be simpler just to enroll him in a good private school, or teach him entirely on your own.

"But I could never teach my own children! It's too hard! So much work!" Not if you know how to multiply your efforts and get rid of educational clutter. More about this in the next chapters.

CHAPTER SEVEN

MULTIPLY AND CONQUER

Y ou are only one person. Now, the problem: how can you be in more than one place at the same time?

If we are going to concentrate on providing *human* education for our children, education that treats them as individuals rather than statistics, we can't always present exactly the same material at exactly the same rate to a mixed group of students. The home teacher, for example, may find herself with an eleven-year-old, a six-year-old, and a two-year-old. Obviously these little people have differing educational needs. The classroom teacher, thanks to peer-group segregation and social promotion, can count on her students sharing the same age; but that is *all* she can count on. One eight-year-old may be capable of teenage work, while another still is shaky on the alphabet. Again, differing educational needs.

Several solutions have been proposed. For home schoolers, integrated curriculum is becoming popular. This is curriculum designed so that the whole family studies the same subject at the same time, but on different levels. You might all journey together to a historic site, for example, and then read books about the history that occurred there. How useful this approach is depends strongly on the ingenuity of the curriculum designers. You can easily obtain general knowledge in this way— each family member grasping what he is able to understand— but basic skills can *not* be taught like this. That is why you always need separate phonics, math, and language arts curriculum to go with your integrated curriculum.

The one-room-schoolhouse method, where the teacher rotates her attention through the classes, each coming forward one at a time to recite and get instruction while the others study and do seatwork, has worked well in America's past. Essential ingredients are (1) a really good teacher and (2) well-behaved students. If the parents or school administration will not allow the teacher to discipline her students effectively, this approach is doomed to fail. It is likewise doomed to fail if the teacher is not quick-minded, able to shift from subject to subject and grade to grade without a hitch. A benefit of the one-room schoolhouse is that students can be at different levels in each subject, thus allowing for more individuality.

You will notice that both these solutions to the problem of one teacher with a group of students with mixed abilities leave *all* the teaching work on the teacher. We're talking hard, hard work here. Integrated curriculum is typically more demanding than other types. The one-room schoolmarm didn't usually dance home at the end of a long school day, either.

Being naturally allergic to hard, hard work, and having a good-sized family of my own, I have long been searching for dodges to get around the pitfalls of one-teacher-bunch-of-kids. Susannah Wesley could teach a dozen of her own children at once, but I'm no Susannah Wesley. And the public schools' "solution" of simply ignoring students' individuality was likewise no option. I *would* be a one-room schoolmarm if I had to— but do I *have* to?

Happily, no. Thanks to the Electronic Age, the Print Age, and a hidden asset to be revealed later, you can enlist dozens of no-cost (or low-cost) tutors to help you out. You can multiply your efforts, and at the same time provide a far richer, individualized education for each of your students. Let's see how it's done.

ARTIFICIAL INTELLIGENCE

Some people think computers will think someday. Silly people. But the electronic family, of which the computer is the most glamorous relative, *can* take a lot of the repetition, drill, and practice of your teaching load off your shoulders— and even present some lessons for you!

Cassettes and Records

I like to read to my children. But (you know how it is) Mom and Dad are not always available to read just when they are wanted. Bingo! Story cassettes! Forget the kind that come with an "educational" read-along book. Kids won't learn to read any quicker from this kind of gimmick. The simple story on cassette is good enough.

What kind of stories are available on cassette? Professionally narrated or acted versions of just about every children's classic, and some you might want to consider as children's classics. Most of us are not capable of doing justice to Shakespeare on our own; but the pros can bring an entire stage production into your home, with no distracting visuals to keep you from eating supper while you listen. Or you can read a story onto cassette (for your personal family use only, of course), to be played back at times when you are not around to read the old favorite.

Music is another natural for your cassette curriculum. Children who listen to a lot of good music played on a particular instrument are much better-prepared to tackle that instrument later on. Your entire family's musical education can also gain in breadth and depth with the addition of a few well-chosen recordings from past eras and other cultures. Folk songs of other countries, and in other languages, can become part of your family's natural environment without any effort on your part. This is a wonderful introduction to social studies.

Memory work can often be helped along by jingles and songs now commercially available. Phonics, math, and even grammar can be learned painlessly by listening to a cassette— and you don't even have to be in the same room as your student!

Instruction for many subjects is also now available on cassette. Foreign language instruction, in particular, is well-suited to this medium. The whole family can listen together, or each student can study a different language at his own pace.

Sources for recordings that do all the above, and more, are written up in *The NEW Big Book of Home Learning* and *The Next Book of Home Learning*.

Videos and Television

Video and television are overrated as educational media. You have to give the visual presentation your entire attention, unlike sound recordings that allow you to knit or eat breakfast while you listen. Television does not allow you to back up and replay a part you didn't understand the first time, unless you have a VCR. Furthermore, both are extremely *slow* ways of presenting data, and both prevent thought and reflection.

Video and TV *are* good at making extremely strong visual impressions. Visual material too dangerous or too inaccessible to approach directly— such as tours of foreign countries or hazardous science experiments— can come across well in these media. Talking heads giving long, boring lectures are a different story.

You can, it is true, import hundreds of teachers into your home or classroom on video. You can even buy an entire video curriculum, almost totally eliminating yourself as a teacher. But the visual media will not make limp presentations more exciting. If anything, the opposite is true. The talking heads from your state university are not likely to hold students' rapt attention.

Showing takes longer than telling, and more money. If the same information is readily available in a book, you are probably wasting your money to invest in a video.

Some people, like cleaning expert Don Aslett, really know how to give an exciting visual presentation. We've played over our *Is There Life After Housework?* video at least a dozen times, and are not tired of it yet. To see an expert *show* you while he tells you can be worth the time and price.

Computers

Computers are the most creative form of artificial teacher, since they can respond (as programmed) to the student. Teaching and feedback occur practically simultaneously. Aha! The Wave of the Future! Computers will take over! Teachers are outmoded!

Not exactly. You can count on your electronic friend to present only what the software geniuses have programmed into him. So your kids can learn electronic engineering with the great *Robot Odyssey* program from Learning Company, but they can't learn simple drawing techniques. Why? Nobody has written a program to teach simple drawing techniques. Until better, cheaper drawing input devices become available, nobody is likely to.

There is no intrinsic reason why computers can't, someday, present lessons with "heart." The programmer is human, and he can put a lot of his humanity into his program. Even so, no computer program is ever going to be able to handle all the unpredictable human responses of your unpredictable human learner.

What computers are great at, right in the here and now, is drill and practice. Computers may sometimes be boring, but they never get bored. Your computer will ask Johnny to add 3+1 for the hundredth time without a hint of impatience. Johnny will not have to chase you all over the house to find out if he is right, either. Furthermore, the drill and practice is likelier more glitzy than what you are able to dish out with homemade flash cards.

What the computer *can't* provide . . . and the video *can't* provide . . . and cassettes and records *can't* provide . . . is human attention and time for reflection. Kids who spend too long sitting in front of computers are living in a world they can totally control, and shut out of the real human world. Thus, some of them grow up to become strange people who can't bear the humanness of other people.

It's fine to mix electronic tutors into your educational program, to provide more personally-tailored instruction than you have time or training for. But they are not *necessary* for a great education. In the wrong hands, these media can be used to eliminate the humanness in teaching and overcontrol what students get in the classroom. That is exactly what is now happening in the American public school system, by the way. You're probably not aware of this, but Secretary of State George Shultz actually signed an agreement to let the Russians and their fellow-traveler American elitists design a soon-to-be-compulsory computer curriculum for all public school grades.[1] (To be compulsory, that is, if we Americans are really so stupid as to passively hand our kids' education over to Soviet propagandists without a struggle.) It's significant that these Brave New Worlders chose a *computer* curriculum to implement their schemes. Parents can look over schoolbooks, and teachers can refuse to teach the lessons as they are dictated by the books. But who can interject one ray of light into the mind of the poor kids locked in front of those computer screens for hours and hours? As the kids are kept busy reacting to the lessons, they won't even have time to *think*.

If electronic media are slated to become the brainwashing tools of choice for those who prefer brainwashing to education, that's one more good reason for the rest of us to find out how to use these tools properly . . . and when *not* to use them.

HUMAN INTELLIGENCE

Every kid should learn how to teach. He should also learn how to teach how to teach. If we ever produce a generation where *nobody* knows how to teach, it's Welcome Dark Ages. If we ever produce a generation where everyone knows how to teach what is good, it's Hello Golden Age!

If you study the history of the biblical nation of Israel, you will find that the reason this nation slid down into idolatry and almost total extinction was that the fathers did not teach their children *to teach their children.* Therefore, teaching our students well is not enough. Even teaching them to teach is not enough. They must be able to teach teaching itself.

Towards this noble end, older children should be involved with the education of the younger children. This is not only necessary for his own education, but an asset to your own teaching efforts. For starters, there is nothing sweeter than a big sister or brother reading to a little sister or brother. Instant multiplication: now there are two or more sources for the little one to beg for a story! Next, they can help drill the youngsters in what they (the oldsters) really know well.

Remember, we are not trying to fool the older ones into thinking they are helping the younger ones so we can sneakily teach the older ones lessons they have missed. Teaching others *has* been shown to help schoolkids remember and understand the lessons they teach. Even so, we are not using the little kids as bait to entice the older kids to learn. We honestly hope and expect that the little kids will learn their lessons while the older ones learn how to teach.

There is more to drill and practice than meets the eye. The older or more accomplished student has to learn how to encourage rather than frustrate, and how to pace the drill and practice. Again, there is nothing sweeter than hearing your son tell his little sister, "That was really good, Sarah. You got almost all of them that time. Are you ready to go through it once more?" The older one learns patience, and the younger one learns.

The next step, teaching a lesson itself, is only possible when the novice teacher really understands how *you* present a lesson. Happily, at home kids are great imitators of their parents. At school, thanks to the way kids are juggled among dozens of teachers over the years, no consistent teaching style may have lodged in their memories. Kids do try to learn how to teach anyway— playing School with littler kids. Watch and see if your kids' idea of teaching is to hand out assignments and criticize, or if they really understand how to explain and respond to questions.

The last stage, teaching how to teach, is passed only when the mature student has passed on to one less advanced the arts of lesson presentation, teaching philosophy, feedback, material selection, and so on. This can't be impossible, or the Lord would not have asked us to do it. The most human way for this to occur is for parents to call on their own parents for advice in the teaching of the young— another action the Bible recommends. Thus, the grandparents continue to train the parents *as teachers* rather than either ignoring their grandchildren's education or bypassing the parents and teaching the grandkids directly. This continuum of teaching needs constantly to be kept up, or the whole process falls to the ground and has to be rebuilt from scratch. But once in place, our civilization can truly continue to build on itself, without throwing out the past and starting each generation from ground zero.

I know of *no* curriculum, Christian or otherwise, which teaches students how to teach. We today find ourselves at that ground zero point of ourselves not having been taught how to teach. Yes, I know there are teachers among us. But what Sunday school program trains parents how to teach their *own* children? How many parents even believe they can train their children in the simplest forms of discipline, let alone teach them to read or write? How many of the best-selling how-to books on "parenting" would sell if parents knew how to teach our own children— and *what* to teach? How many teachers would put up with the twaddle foisted on them as "curriculum" if *they* knew how to teach? How could the entire Special Education complex even survive if teachers dared to take responsibility for actually teaching their students, instead of labeling the *students* as mental cripples?

Any attempt at all you make in the direction of teaching your students how to teach will be a service, not only to them, but through them, to all mankind.

I FOUND IT IN A BOOK

We sometimes talk of a student studying books on his own as "self-instruction." Nothing could be farther from the truth! The child or adult alone with a book is actually getting instruction from another human being— the book's author. Furthermore, this instruction is swifter than oral instruction, easier to review, and ideally suited to the disciplines of studying, thinking, comparing, and imagining.

Captain Eddie Rickenbacker, the great World War I flying Ace of Aces who took Eastern Airlines from a cash drain to the only airline profitable on its own without government subsidies, was a seventh-grade dropout. Eddie loved cars and wanted to learn auto mechanics. With his educational background, though, no college would take him. But that was before young Eddie started his program of self-improvement with the help of correspondence courses and books.

> The first lesson, I do not mind admitting, nearly finished my correspondence-school education before it began. It was tough, and I was a little rusty when it came to formal education. I had to teach myself to study all over again, and, furthermore, I had to teach myself to think. I did not realize then, as I laboriously worked away at the lessons all alone, that I was receiving a greater benefit from them than I would have received from the same courses in a classroom. As there was no teacher of whom I could ask an explanation, I had to work out the answers myself. *Once I reached the answer through my own individual reasoning, my understanding was permanent and unforgettable.* (Emphasis mine.)[2]

The type of book the student is left alone with is, of course, essential. More than eighty years ago, British educator Charlotte Mason was already complaining bitterly about "lesson books with pretty pictures and easy talk" which she astutely named "little pills of knowledge in the form of a weak and copious diluent." Susan Schaeffer Maculay, a Charlotte Mason disciple, pinpoints part of the problem, especially as it relates to literature. Children are given "little snippets of information here and there" rather than being allowed to work through a complete book.

> Children benefit from working steadily through a well-chosen book. And if they narrate it to you, it will become theirs. But more happens. Because they've tackled a complete book, they become acquainted with its flow and its use of language. They are students of another person—the author. Further, they are allowed to notice the content themselves. As they aren't forced to memorize facts, they are free to react to the writing themselves. They are the ones who determine what parts they consider important. It becomes an active experience of the mind, personality, and language.[3]

Richard Mitchell, the Underground Grammarian, brings us up-to-date with his equally bitter complaint about how schoolbook publishers have almost completely stifled the possibility of student interaction with an individual author.

> A book is the permanent record of the work of a solitary human mind, to be read, marked, learned, and inwardly digested by another solitary human mind. A committee can no more make a book than it can play the violin, but almost every "book" used in schools—and in teacher-training academies—is written collectively and for collective purposes.
>
> A magnificent education, as countless examples attest, can come from nothing more than reading and writing. In the one we behold the work of the solitary mind, in the other we do it, but we do it in such a way that we can behold again, and understand, and judge, the work of a solitary mind—our own. . . But the gimmickry of the schools . . . is an integral and large portion of *a general program designed to prevent solitude.* And while the children themselves are pestered with values clarification modules and relating sessions and group activities lest they fall into solitude, they are also protected from dangerous exposure to the fruits of solitary thinking in others. (Emphasis mine.)[4]

Allan Bloom, author of the best-seller *Closing of the American Mind,* explains that a great problem of our current culture, "the decay of the family's traditional role as the transmitter of tradition," has the same root as the decay of the humanities: "nobody believes that the old books do, or even could, contain the truth."[5] Here he exaggerates, as Bible-believing Christians, to name just one group, *do* believe in absolute truths taught in ancient books. If we agree with Bloom, as I do, that the family *must* keep itself "distinct from the popular culture" and pass judgment on the fads of the times rather than be swallowed up by them, then it is vital that our children get their hands on books *not* written by card-carrying members of the currently fashionable elite.

So good books are more than wonderful, free tutors for your students. It is true that children who have learned to love reading can be settled down with a good book in the same way less-astute parents plop them in front of the television baby-sitter. You can gain immense peace and quiet by well-timed library trips, and have the satisfaction that your student is doing "something worthwhile" in the corner with a book while you concentrate on teaching his classmates or siblings (or knitting, or taking a nap). But books are more than helpers. If I can put it this strongly, it is our *duty* to let the great writers and thinkers of the past tutor our children, before the less-great writers and thinkers of today simply capture them with slogans.

Practically no school today gives books their proper role. The undisturbed mind-to-mind contact with a great mind; the enjoyment of solitude; the training in thinking and discernment; the wide experience of other cultures and other times are almost totally submerged in a round of incessant busyness. You, at home with your children, or behind your classroom door, can make this one most significant change all by yourself. Read to your children until they develop the true "reading readiness" of being able to follow a story, and do this whether they are two or twelve. Teach them to read, if they do not know how (it takes about twenty hours with intensive phonics: see sources in *The NEW Big Book of Home Learning*). Then *give them books—not* just the currently popular ones, but *old* books supposedly "too hard" for them— and *let them alone.* This one simple thing will schoolproof your children more thoroughly than any other.

I will have much more to say on the subject of books and schools in Chapter 12. For now, just consider this proposal: *A well-rounded education should include not only solitary reading in literature, but self-study from course books.* The student who has learned how to study on his own has really learned how to learn. Don't be too anxious to baby your good readers along. Let them struggle a bit. Give them assignments to complete on their own. If one comes asking for help, give a hint if you must, but encourage him to try a bit longer and see if he can solve the problem on his own. This builds the habit of independence. *Use* books as your fellow teachers!

CHAPTER EIGHT

EDUCATIONAL CLUTTER'S LAST STAND

Getting the clutter out of your life can and will rid you of more discouragement, tiredness, and boredom than anything else you can do.

Don Aslett, author of the book *Clutter's Last Stand*

braham Lincoln's nose. Educational clutter. What do these have in common? Not much, except that I am now looking at the cover of a popular teacher's magazine. This particular cover shows a workman suspended in the blue sky near the right nostril of the granite face of President Lincoln on Mt. Rushmore. An odd beginning for an issue dedicated to a "Presidential Salute."

But Abraham Lincoln's nose has at least as much to do with a Presidential Salute as most of the clever "educational" material within this— and every other— teacher's magazine has to do with education. Along with the usual glitzy full-page ads from major curriculum publishers whose advertising agencies seem to be competing for the Vapid Slogan of the Year Award, the reader is flooded with brilliant ideas for doing silly things. A mere sampling from this one issue:

- A "Success in Reading and Writing" program that forces children to do all the following when studying the letter D: give the teacher words that use the "D" sound; recite funny "D" words; copy those words from a chart the teacher makes; break into groups to discuss them; and then on the *next* day "expand the D words into two- and three-word phrases and again discuss the words in groups"; "thumb through magazines, newspapers and unusual books to find other D words"; all culminating in the giddy pleasure of seeing these new words "on charts which grace the classroom walls as the class progresses to the letter E." This educational breakthrough came from a school featured in the "A+ Schools" section of the magazine.

- An aptly named "Read-iculous Read-a-thon" featuring such essential educational events as Really Ridiculous Reader's Day (kids bring odd things to read to school—"some even wear swimsuits and do their reading seated on an inner tube"), a Read-iculous Pep Rally where "children use their bodies to form letters while cheering," and What a Character! Day where "students and teachers dress as their favorite book characters and parade through the school while others try to guess who they portray."

- A George Washington hat wig made of construction paper. Not too bad so far, but the inventor warns it could lead to trouble: "You'll plan a George Washington play just to use this clever hat/wig combo."

- This one speaks for itself. "Beg or borrow a pair of huge shoes (size 16, bright and colorful preferred). Search the school for someone to fill them. Chances are you'll fail, but students will increase communication along the way . . . Encourage suggestions as to who would wear the shoes. Try them on. Take pictures. Write stories about them. Post stories and pictures outside the classroom to involve and arouse questions from other classes . . . "[1]

I give up. What do big feet have to do with education? You give up, too? Good. There is hope for both of us.

I wonder if it ever occurs to the people who write the bulging Teacher's Manuals, and the clever curriculum enhancers, and the geniuses who come up with ideas like Communication with Big Feet, that they are just creating busywork for teachers and students. I further wonder if they realize that all this raging ocean of cleverness is threatening to completely flood out *true* education. After all, you can't spend hours searching your school for big-footed students *and* read Shakespeare at the same time. You can't be putting on a play about George Washington just to try out your new hat wigs in public *and* learning fractions at the same time. (Don't kid yourself about how educational it would be for students to write such a play either. The whole thing will get "broken down into groups" so no individual will have any real hand in any significant playwriting, and the teacher will end up writing most of it.)

Let's get really educational for a minute. Let's talk about cost/benefit ratios. A cost/benefit ratio is the ratio between what something costs and the benefit you receive from it. For example, if you buy a used car for $1,000 and get 50,000 miles out of it without need for major maintenance, your cost/benefit ratio would be $1 per 50 miles driven. If you buy a new car for $10,000 and get 100,000 miles out of it, the cost/benefit ratio would be $1 per 10 miles driven. Now, to save money, which car would be the better deal? Right— the used car! This simplistic example leaves out factors like gas mileage, driving comfort, trade-in value, pride of ownership, and so on. Still, you get the idea. Products can be compared in terms of costs and benefits.

Let's now apply cost/benefit ratios to education. *How does the amount of time spent teaching children compare to the actual educational benefit they receive?*

Going back to our examples up above: The "Success in Reading and Writing Program" takes two days to introduce one letter. Cost/benefit: 2 days/letter. In contrast, the typical intensive phonics program takes 20 hours of instruction to teach children *everything* they need to be able to read. Cost/benefit: Just a few hours/all 26 letters. The "Read-iculous Read-a-thon" takes an entire class day, plus preparation, to get across the idea that books are not the only thing you can read. If this point were not already obvious to every child who eats breakfast cereal, two minutes of normal class time should have sufficed. The George Washington Hat Wig Project, a more modest proposal, will probably take a half-hour of class time, plus preparation and clean-up. The benefit here is (1) children learn that George Washington wore a hat and wig and (2) they get to play with construction paper. The play part is fun— I'll give it that— but if the pseudo-historic focus on President Washington makes this *educational*, I'll eat my hat-wig. Finally, Communication with Big Feet. First the teacher has to find a pair of size 16 shoes, "bright and colorful preferred." This alone could take several days of intensive shopping. Maybe she has to *buy* these unwearable shoes. Educational value so far: nil. Cost: up to $75 bucks (colorful size 16s aren't cheap, you know!). The entire school then gets to waste hours playing Cinderella with these enormous shoes (educational value, still nil). "Encourage suggestions as to who would wear the shoes." The imaginative value of this exercise:

less than reading *Jack in the Beanstalk.* "Try them on." A few laughs for comic relief. "Take pictures." A waste of good film. "Write stories about them." Ah, now we're *really* getting educational! Of course, the children could have written ten stories by now about far more interesting and important subjects. "Post stories and pictures outside the classroom to involve and arouse questions from other classes." A great idea, this. Now the entire school can be distracted from real education to ponder the deeper meaning of big feet.

❧ ❧ ❧ ❧ ❧ ❧ ❧ ❧ ❧

You feel guilty, don't you? Guilty because you can't ever seem to get through *all* the adorable enrichment ideas in the Teacher's Manual. Guilty because *your* bulletin boards aren't fresh every week, like the dedicated scissors-wielder's down the hall. Guilty because your poor, deprived students don't have all the latest educational software . . . have never built an entire urban renewal project out of shoeboxes . . . have never written a Class Book about big feet. Life is so short, and our students, alas, are missing *so much!*

So we fill our bulging files full of clever ideas that exhaust us. Teach phonics with macaroni chains? Bake a real pie and let the class cut it up for fraction practice? Collect tin cans so our darlings can make them into astronauts and simulate the Moon Landing? Let's *do* it! This will be *creative!* But, alas, we can't do it *all.* And meanwhile our pie-fed and macaroni-draped students seem awfully short of time for those little things like Reading and Writing and are awfully far behind in Arithmetic.

The night is dark, brothers and sisters. Let's quietly slip our chains while nobody is watching. A quick slither into the thickets, a flutter of all that other lovely educational clutter into the friendly waters of the nearest river, and nobody will be able to catch us. You'll feel at least fifty pounds lighter . . .

CURRICULUM CLUTTER

The secret is out— the better teacher you get to be, the less you will need expensive curriculum and supplies. A beginning teacher can teach all her children to read with a prepackaged curriculum, and have them reading years ahead in six months or less. A good teacher can teach phonics with a few simple readers, flash cards, and a chalkboard. A great teacher can do it with library books and a pencil and ten sheets of paper! The difference is simply that the great teacher knows exactly where she is going and how to handle each roadblock or opportunity along the way.

This doesn't mean that the sign of a great teacher is a bare classroom with no educational games or chalkboard. Once upon a time these teachers probably bought *more* new products than we did. What distinguishes them from the rest of us is that they had the courage to heave stuff that didn't work. They know how to separate the wheat from the chaff.

First, curriculum clutter. Let's take phonics as our example. After having reviewed more than two dozen phonics programs, I am continually amazed at the new, imaginative ways people dream up to make this simple process complicated.

Cute Doesn't Get to the Root

Some phonics programs get cute. They dress up the letters like little animals or little people. The little animals or little people each have their own adorable little story or little song to help your children remember the animal or person forever. Problem is, you're not trying to teach your students about aardvarks or Amy. You're trying (aren't you?) to teach the letter A. Of course, if you *want* to teach elementary zoology or present character lessons *instead of* teaching reading, that's a different story.

The Fifty Nifties

Another typical dodge is the Fifty Nifties. Your Teacher's Manual, you find as you struggle the twenty-pound monster open, comes with fifty nifty activities at the end of each and every lesson. Often these activities are only loosely connected with the lesson concept. (Sometimes the *lesson* is only loosely connected with the lesson concept, but we'll get to that later.) In any case, the Fifty Nifties are designed to help classroom teachers fill up those dreaded empty hours. Smart classroom teachers know enough to ignore most of this stuff. The world, they reason, will not end if every child whose name begins in B misses out on a chance to march to the front of the room and see his name written on the blackboard. Home schoolers, however, tend to fall apart, believing that children in school are actually doing all these marvelous activities, and dying of frustration because they are unable to do likewise. (If your only child's name is Clarence that means there is *nobody* to march to the blackboard for letters A, B, and D-Z.)

Red Herrings

Red herrings also swarm in these waters. What does a child learn from doing hundreds of pages of workbook exercises on a few phonograms? He learns how to do a bunch of strange exercises, that's what. He even gets so involved in learning how to do these strange exercises that he forgets he is studying phonics. That's the genius of "phony phonics" courses. They keep you so busy that you never notice nobody is learning to read.

SPOTTING CURRICULUM CLUTTER BEFORE IT STOPS YOU!

You can identify curriculum clutter by asking a few simple questions:

1. *What* am I trying to teach?
2. Is it *worth it?*
3. Does what I am doing *match the goal?*
4. Is what I am doing *worth the time* it takes?

If I am trying to teach fractions, why am I baking a pie? Maybe I'm not *really* trying to teach fractions. I am only using fractions as an excuse for teaching cooking, and for getting to eat a pie. That's OK, and now that I recognize this I will make sure that I don't fall into the habit of pie-baking every time fractions come up. There are less time-consuming ways of teaching fractions, and as far as teaching addition of fractions with different denominators, pies are out. So I will *not* base my fractions curriculum on pies.

I find myself trying to teach a lesson on Valentine's Day. Now, exactly how much time is this worth? A day? A week? An hour? Maybe we'll just make valentines and forget the heart-shaped bulletin board and heart cookies and all the other trivia that we could so easily spend our time on.

The honest truth is that much of the stuff taught in the schools is not worth teaching; much of what remains misses the goal; and much of the rest takes far more time than it's worth. As Don Aslett points out:

The well-known 80/20 rule of business says: If all of a given category of items are sorted in order of value, 80 percent of the value will come from only 20 percent of the items. Think about that in terms of clutter. Eighty percent of the space on our shelves (and in our mind) is occupied by stuff we never need. . . . [2]

In modern education, the problem is that the 20 percent of valuable teaching is being overwhelmed by the 80 percent of useless curriculum clutter. In the resulting confusion, kids are hard-pressed to hang on to even the 20 percent. I am not pleading for 100 percent efficiency, just first things first. If the kids are reading well and are up to snuff in math and so on, if they want to make George Washington Hat Wigs in their spare time, who am I to spoil their fun? But if they are going to make Hat Wigs *instead* of learning to read and write, it's time to hide the construction paper.

LEARNING BY MOOING

An idea is making the rounds, particularly in integrated curriculum circles, that children learn best by doing. In other words, to learn about cows, *be* a cow. Moo, walk around on all fours, and pretend to eat grass.

The superiority of learning-by-doing is at best a half-truth. Children remember better what they have experienced themselves— but given only so many hours in a day, children learn *less* when they are required to "experience" rather than simply study new material. Hands-on experiments, role-playing, and field trips all take *much* more time than reading, listening to lectures, and other traditional forms of learning.

If every new bit of learning has to be "experienced," then children will spend their days designing and making Hat Wigs rather than reading the biography of George Washington. They will spend weeks simulating the lifestyles of the Plains Indians rather than covering the hundreds of years of American history. The time given to one "enriching" activity is time taken from solid study. Worse, if a family should miss its field trip to Gettysburg (perhaps the family lives in Puerto Rico), they will have missed out on *really* learning about the Civil War . . . since learning about that sort of thing from mere books is only a second-hand, vastly inferior, somewhat suspect approach.

Experience-based learning is generally only simulations anyway, since most field trip sites are inaccessible to most of us. We can't visit Iran to learn about the Iranians, which would be *true* experience-based learning. To dress up as Iranians and eat an Iranian meal is not quite the same as being there. However, this sort of "lesson" *does* present a mirage of "understanding" Iranians and enable secularized Westerners to keep that treasured belief in the alikeness and equal goodness of all cultures and religions. Social relativity is hard to teach with *real* "real-world" experiences, but easy with learning-by-doing simulations.

Enrichment activities can be just that— enrichment— or they can become a subtle form of censorship, preserving the student from ever having to touch reality. If we kid ourselves into thinking we "studied" George Washington just because we now know he wore a powdered wig, we are apt to forget that we still know nothing about what George said and precious little about what he did.

A textbook-based curriculum must include some basic information, or its defection from knowledge will be too obvious. Responsible writers of integrated curriculum include many books in their programs so children can obtain that basic knowledge, perhaps from better sources than a textbook. This basic knowledge is the essential part of the curriculum. The rest is extra— and if you don't really want to do it, pitch it.

RUBE GOLDBERG CURRICULUM

Rube Goldberg, an American cartoonist, became famous for his cartoons of zany "inventions." The typical Rube Goldberg invention takes something simple, like making pancakes, and turns it into a complicated process. A gun fired by remote action startles a bird from its perch, thus tilting a lever, thus starting a pancake-mixing machine, into which flour pours from a hole in a bag nibbled by a mouse . . . etc. In theory, the invention might work— but only if you want to take the time to capture birds and mice, rig levers and pulleys, purchase guns and corks to shoot out of guns, and in general take a week to perform a simple five-minute action.

In the rush to incorporate hands-on instruction and learning-by-doing, some of what emerges looks an awful lot like Rube Goldberg's inventions. I'll give you an only slightly exaggerated case:

"Start a stuffed elephant collection. This teaches zoology . . . taxidermy . . . household storage methods . . . and camping."

"Camping?"

"Yes! When your elephant collection begins to fill your whole bedroom, you will have to camp out on the living room sofa, thus learning valuable survival skills."

How to Invent Your Own Rube Goldberg Project

Here's how to invent your own Rube Goldberg project. Incidentally, here's also how to spot this kind of project.

1. Pick an activity . . . any activity.
2. Figure out what "skills" this activity employs.
   a. Basic skills: matching, sorting, classifying, recognizing colors and shapes, and so on.

b. Thinking skills: comparing, analyzing, observing, deducing . . .

c. Physical skills: hand-eye coordination (almost *every* project involves this skill!), balance, fine motor skills, gross motor skills.

d. Other skills: telephone skills, use and care of tools, social interaction skills . . .

3. Figure out what subjects this project can be attached to.

a. Animal, vegetable, or mineral? If it involves any of these, call it science.

b. Communication: if it involves reading, writing, speaking, listening, or watching TV, call it language arts.

c. People: if they come into it at all (as in making a play dough model of Mommy), call it social studies.

d. Fictional people: now it's language arts and literature.

e. Does this project involve more than one of anything? Does the student have to count, add, subtract, multiply, or divide? Even if the math involved is no more than dividing the play dough into two equal lumps, you can say this project "involves math skills."

f. Arts and crafts: if you use *colored* pencils, you can call it art. Any kind of art or craft media or technique used, including stickers, makes it art.

g. Music: humming, singing, chanting, listening to recordings, banging with chopsticks on pot lids . . .

h. Engineering/design: any use of construction kits.

i. Social skills: any time two kids get together.

j. Survival skills: everything kids normally learn at home without making a big deal out of it, like how to answer the telephone and how to cross the street.

k. Self-image: knowing your body parts and believing you are unique and wonderful. The latter comes built-in, but curriculum designers spend hundreds of hours "teaching" it anyway.

4. Now, list all the skills and subjects you can think of.
5. What would be the consequences of the child learning all this? For example, if he learns to saw wood, he will get good exercise. List the consequences.
6. Also the consequences of the consequences. If he gets good exercise, he may go out for sports. Carry this as far as you can manage.

To show how this works: take our example of modeling Mommy out of play dough. The student is using the basic skill of color recognition (choosing which colors of play dough to use), observing (what does Mommy look like?), and the physical skills of hand-eye coordination and fine motor skills (squishing the dough). If she tells you about her Mommy-lump, that's communication skills. Mommy herself is part of "the family," an important social studies concept. If she counts two arms and two legs, that is math. Art is involved, of course, as is self-image ("I am Mommy's little girl"). The consequence of making the play dough model will be that she will have to decide whether to save it or throw it out (higher level thinking skills: decision strategies). If she throws it out, she can practice household sanitation by throwing it in the trash bucket rather than on the floor. If she saves it, she can practice organizing skills (where will she put it?). If Mommy disagrees with her choice, it's an opportunity to practice communication, logic, argumentation, and running. And so on.

You will notice that most of the "skills" practiced in our example normally are used by human beings every day. Just as Rube Goldberg's inventions showed us how to make everyday activities complicated, so this type of project approach shows us how to make everyday activities into mystical educational processes.

Underlying all this is the not-so-subtle idea that people *only* learn by doing activities prescribed by others. *Those* activities then are educational, and worth wasting years of students' time on.

The trademark of Rube Goldberg projects is that *students aren't really taught enough of any given skill or subject to make a difference.* Counting two arms and two legs is a two-second math input. Modeling Mommy teaches almost nothing about the family. The amount of practice in hand-eye coordination from making one play dough model can't make any significant difference to a child's physical abilities. Sure, kids "do" all the subjects and skills listed, but they don't *learn* any of them.

In our example of modeling Mommy, the one *real* skill or subject that can be taught is sculpture. A knowledgeable teacher or parent can lead the child to observe better, notice proportion, become comfortable with the medium, and actually improve artistically with a series of such models. As far as communication skills, social studies, math, and so on, forget it.

The answer to Rube Goldberg projects, then, is to

1. Identify the *real* subject or skill being taught.
2. Ask, "Is there, or can there be, sufficient teaching input on that skill or subject to actually teach the student something significant?"
3. Ask, " Is the subject or skill worth teaching?"

Eliminate the clutter of trying to teach a hundred phony skills and subjects and concentrate on the *real* skills the project teaches.

This Is Organized?

Another Rube Goldberg approach, widely used in integrated curriculum programs (programs that try to "integrate" knowledge rather than teaching it as separate subjects) is the odd grouping of curriculum topics.

If you are going to produce a curriculum, you have to organize it somehow. If you are not going to systematically study Human Anatomy as part of a separate Science course, you will have to figure out where Human Anatomy comes into your organizing scheme.

That is why we see strange groupings like Attentiveness (character theme), Ear (because we listen attentively with our ear), Music (because we hear music with our attentive ears), and Symphony (because it's a form of music); or Jacob's journey to Egypt by camel train with Transportation (camel trains are transportation). These groupings are totally artificial.

A problem arises when the curriculum purchaser feels he *must* teach the Ear now because it's right there in the manual. A study of the Ear is not intrinsic to the study of attentiveness or the study of music. Attentiveness itself may not be a fit study for several months of classroom study (I strongly suspect this). Happily, the better integrated curricula cheat by covering many areas in chronological order, even though the chronology may have nothing to do with their organizing scheme.

The way to handle this is to go through the manual crossing out the units you feel are superfluous or silly (e.g., a detailed study of the seating arrangement of a symphony orchestra when you have never even attended the symphony in your life). You then have to go through the remaining units crossing out superfluous or silly projects. Determine if what is left is worth the time to teach it. Are you still stuck with two weeks' worth of lessons on the Ear? Then whittle it down to two or three good projects, like drawing or constructing an ear model and some experiments with tuning forks. Never mind about the twenty other darling projects in the Ear unit. You can always do them next year if you feel like it.

If all this is too much work, stick with textbooks and library books and the encyclopedia.

Figuring out the Areas

Some areas just need to be taught systematically. Math, for example. As we have seen, we can play with pies as an *introduction* to fractions, but when it comes to serious multiplying, dividing, adding, and subtracting, pie math is time-consuming, messy, and basically unsuited to getting across these concepts.

Sometimes publishers of Rube Goldberg curriculum try to kid you along about all the "math experiences" and "language experiences" children are getting in their programs. What they are *really* doing is mushing isolated math and language fragments into totally unrelated activities. They are cluttering the curriculum with bits of math and language arts, and simultaneously obscuring math and language. Nobody *needs* to visit a carpet showroom to practice calculating area. This is curriculum clutter.

GROUP CLUTTER

In my dear old junior high days, I took a Home Ec course. There were four kitchens and thirteen girls. To ensure that each girl had something to do, every recipe got broken down into itsy-bitsy parts. For example, to make scrambled eggs, Margie would get out the eggs, Ruth would crack them into a bowl, Kathy would stir them, and Amy would grease the pan and cook the eggs. The time not spent working felt like playing outer right field; you stood around hoping one of the real players would get sidelined so you could get back into the game.

The Home Ec teachers had a reason— insufficient kitchen space— for making us do everything in teams. True, it did make Home Ec excruciatingly boring, but that wasn't their fault.

Today, it's a different story. Everything from writing papers to cleaning the blackboards becomes a group activity. A law seems to have been passed against children learning or doing anything on their own. This is clutter and a waste of time. So are the endless discussions and rap sessions where kids practice groupthink while pondering subjects of which they as yet know nothing, and teachers practice group manipulation while pretending to want to find out the students' opinions. Rare indeed is the teacher who lets kids say what they actually *think*, instead of guiding them to the One Right Answer in the Teacher's Manual. Rarer still is the occasion where the entire class actually needs to know what everyone else in the class opines on a subject. Rarest of all is the case when all this tongue-wagging beats a good session of Parchesi for educational value.

TEACHER CLUTTER

Some are born clutterers. Some achieve clutterhood. Others have clutterhood thrust upon them . . .

One problem with knowing how to teach is that you can *always* think of ten different ways to complicate a perfectly simple lesson. Just look at the chapter in this book on Twenty Ways to Present a Lesson. The clever teacher is not stuck simply reciting "Columbus sailed the ocean blue/In fourteen hundred ninety-two." No, no! We know about *dressing up* like Columbus, or *making models* of the Niña, Pinta and Santa Maria. We can *watch a video* on ocean travel, or fill a jar with blue water and *float little ships* in it. The class can *break up into small groups and discuss* Columbus' voyage, or *pretend* they are sailing with Columbus. Everyone can make *maps* of the voyage and *give presentations*. Etc.

Your job, should you choose to accept it, is to pick the simplest way to present a given lesson and stick to it. *After* the kids get the lesson down, if you all want to play for a while and if it would make you feel too guilty just to go outside and swing on the swing set, you can try out all those clever but only marginally lesson-related arts and crafts and drama ideas.

Clutter can be fun, in its place. But it NEVER should be allowed to crowd out actual learning. Decorate your lessons as much as you and your students like. But please, let's give them a real cake with a little frosting, rather than a lot of frosting on a hollow cardboard tube.

PART III

PERSONALITY IS BEAUTIFUL

CHAPTER NINE

SQUARE PEGS AND PIGEONHOLES

W e're sitting at the supper table. The baby is yelling. He is not hungry or thirsty. We know this because he is throwing his food and cup on the floor. He is bored. Happily, I know what to do. I will cheer up the baby by distracting him. My hand becomes a spider, creeping up his arm. "Itsy, bitsy spider, climbing up the spout . . . " The baby is cheered up.

Meanwhile, at the dinner table behind my back, spiders are congregating. Especially one big hairy one, otherwise known as my husband Bill's hand. It comes creeping at *me* as I turn around to grab a bite of food. Eek! I mush the "spider" down with my left hand and pound on it with my right. The spider flops a few times, twitches theatrically, and dies. "I had no choice," I explain to Bill. "It was the only merciful thing to do." We all bellow with laughter.

Queen Victoria, I bet, never had to squash Prince Albert's imaginary spiders. If she did, I can't imagine her *laughing* about it. But then, I will never have to be Queen of England and set the cultural tone for an empire. Neither will I ever have to be a World War I flying ace like Eddie Rickenbacker, or a daring reporter like Nellie Bly, or a model of taciturnity like Calvin Coolidge. And that's not all bad. We can't *all* be ace pilots, or reporters, or Strong Silent Men.

Modern education generally does recognize that people are different. In fact, starting in preschool we get the "I am so special! I am wonderful!" treatment. Problem is, this encouraging litany does not mean what it says. It does not mean that children are unique human beings created in the image of God, each with his own personality, talents, and tendencies to sin. As we proceed through the grades we discover these same "special" and "wonderful" children forced into peer-group herds. The energetic are labeled "hyperactive" and sedated. The slow-and-steadies are labeled "learning disabled" and shunted into Special Ed. The mean and destructive are not told to shape up or ship out, but labeled "emotionally handicapped" and coddled. Solitary types who hate the group pressures and inanity of school schedules are labeled "school phobic" and granted no concessions to their sensitive natures.

The bottom line of all this, you will notice, is that children are forced to *fit in* to the school. Kids who don't fit in are *forced* in. Square pegs in round holes. Hard on the square pegs, and not too great on the round holes, either.

Could it be that highly critical people, and aggressive people, and slow methodical people, and humorous people all have a *right* to their own personalities? Can it be OK for students to be human not only in how they learn and are motivated, but in their different personalities as well? Could we perhaps get a nice big garbage can and place all those hundreds of little labels out on the curb for the trashman to take away?

ONE SIZE FITS NONE

Let's look for a minute at the ways people are different.
Leaving aside good and bad character traits at the moment,
you can be:

- Quiet or outgoing
- Sensitive or unflappable
- Methodical or given to spurts of energy
- Serious or humorous
- Moody or optimistic
- Idealistic or practical
- Full of energy or sedentary

You can see these personality types, and many more, in
mere babies. Some babies take setbacks much harder than
others. Some babies are much more fascinated with doorknobs
and take-apart toys than others. I've seen big placid babies
and small energetic babies and people-loving babies and quiet
babies and methodical babies and rollicking babies. This does
not mean that the methodical baby will never act on impulse,
or the placid baby won't get all fired up when someone
repeatedly steals his toys—just that we each have leanings in
certain directions built into our very natures.

The purpose of education is *not* "to train children to fit into
society." This is Robot Education, not people education. Our
job is *not* to homogenize all children into one easy-to-mold
mass. Anyway, that's been tried—for fifty years!—and it still
isn't working. Kids *are* human, and human beings will *never* fit
into the same little box.

Christianity teaches that we must deny ourselves and
strive to become more like Jesus. This means, usually, that we
must deny our corrupt tendencies, not that we must deny our

basic personalities. The time may come, it is true, when the meek and quiet (like Moses) has to call up his courage and face the public, or the fiery type (like Jonah) has to settle for God blessing his enemies instead of calling down doom upon them. In our eventual callings we may need enough courage to do what goes against the grain of our natural selves. But our *education* is not supposed to violate the personalities God gave us! Jesus, in the three and a half years He spent with His disciples, did not turn out twelve Peters or twelve Johns. Each of those men came out of his training period *more* of what he went in. Peter was *more* courageous, John *more* spiritual-minded, and Paul the Apostle, who received his teaching directly from the risen Lord, was *more* of an excellent arguer and scholar when Jesus had trained him.

If we can learn to think of students as *people*, each with his or her unique contribution to give the world— which may include being the one who does *not* fit in to society, but instead helps *change* society— then we will realize we have an obligation to treat each one differently. One moral rule fits all— e.g., "Thou shalt not smite thy classmate"— but one academic rule never will fit all. We must try to quench those little twinges of wishing Johnny were more like Suzy, who sits so nicely and quietly. Students are all different . . . but would you really want a classroom of robots?

Vive la différence!

CHAPTER TEN

LEARNING THAT FITS

*"I may not know much . . .
but I SUSPECT a lot of things!"*

Junior Semples

O K. We're going to celebrate children's differences and teach to their differences. But what can we give each child that is special?

We can't waive the moral rules, or show favoritism in dishing out rewards and sanctions. That's out. What we can do is:

• Recognize children's different learning styles

• Adjust the content of teaching to their roles and talents, and, to a lesser extent, their interests

• Adjust the speed of teaching

• Not penalize children for their legitimate differences—e.g., by grades and labeling

THANK HEAVEN FOR LEARNING STYLES

Lots has been written about learning styles— more than I have patience to read. Everyone is busy inventing his own terminology and "discovering" hundreds of new styles, some of which (each hopes) will make useful replacements for the current negative special ed labels. New pigeonholes are being developed, in other words, but it's still Pigeonhole City.

Do not worry about all this research. Basically, learning styles break down into input/output styles (ways kids take in and demonstrate knowledge) and thinking styles.

Thinking styles are both inaccessible and none of our business. All we need be concerned with at the moment is the ways kids learn and demonstrate their learning.

God gave you four main ways to take in data:

- Through your eyes (visual learning)

- Through your ears (auditory learning)

- Through your sense of touch (tactile learning)

- Through movement (kinesthetic learning)

To this we could add one more: you can be born knowing it. Plato pointed out that kids are able to extrapolate from the sight of one chair to recognize chairs of completely different styles. Therefore, he reasoned, babies must be born with an understanding of "Universals" and the ability to classify even brand-new objects. We are also born with an interest in other people and with inbuilt learning methods. Nobody has to teach a baby to take in data! This is part of what it means to be made in the image of God. Thus, even people whose sensory and mental apparatus is highly deficient can think and learn. Our job is (1) to believe in our students' built-in human spirits and (2) to make the most of their existing sensory channels and learning styles, while gently building up new learning paths, if possible.

Visual Learners

Are you easily distracted by new sights? Do you remember where you put things? Are you good at catching typos and doing puzzles? Are you very aware of visual details in drawings? Do you remember names better when you see them on a name tag? If you answered "yes" to these questions, you are a *visual* learner.

Visual learners need to *see* what they are supposed to do. You should write out a model, or demonstrate visually the skill to be learned. Some materials that are good for visual learners are:

a. flash cards
b. matching games
c. puzzles
d. instruction books
e. charts
f. pictures, posters, wall strips, desk tapes

Auditory Learners

Do you like to talk a lot? Do you talk to yourself? As a child, were you a "babbler"? Do you remember names easily? Can you carry a tune? Do you like to "keep the beat" along with the music? Do you read out loud or subvocalize during reading? Can you follow oral directions more easily than written directions? When taking tests, do you frequently know the answer, but have trouble expressing it on paper? Then you are an *auditory* learner.

Auditory learners learn best by hearing. They need to be *told* what to do. Auditory learners will listen to you reading for hours, but you may not think they are paying attention because they don't look at you. They like to memorize by ear and can easily develop a good sense of rhythm. Naturally, auditory learners have a head start when it comes to learning music. Good materials for auditory learners are:

    a. cassette tapes
    b. educational songs and rhymes (like the "ABC Song")
    c. rhythm instruments

Tactile/Kinesthetic Learners

Now for the physical types! Here are your so-called "hyperactives." As a child, did you have difficulty sitting still? Were you always grabbing for things? Did you always run your finger across the boards when walking past a fence? Do you move around a lot, and use animated gestures and facial expressions when talking? Can you walk along the curb without losing your balance? Do you prefer hugs from your spouse rather than verbal praise? Do you like to take things apart? Are you always fooling with paper or something on your desk when you're on the phone? If so, then you're a *kinesthetic* learner.

Hands-on learning is a must for kinesthetic learners. They need to mold or sculpt or whittle or bend, fold, and mutilate in order to express themselves. Kinesthetic learners learn to read best by learning to write. They like math manipulatives and sandpaper letters. Kinesthetic learners do *not* like sitting at a desk for hours staring at the blackboard— it's like blindfolding a visual learner to do this to a kinesthetic learner.

For kinesthetic learners, try:

a. long nature walks
b. model kits
c. yard work and gardening
d. textured puzzles
e. typing instead of writing (it's faster and less frustrating)

Be sure to have kinesthetic learners write BIG when they are first learning. Large muscle action zips through to the brain more easily than small, fine movements. Manipulative materials and a good phonics program cure reversals in kinesthetic learners, who are the group most frequently labeled "dyslexic."

Schoolproofing with Learning Styles

Your learning style is also probably your teaching style. Auditory learners love to lecture, and visual learners like to give reading assignments and prepare visual aids. Tactile/kinesthetic learners are likely to be gym coaches and crafts teachers.

A problem arises when the teacher's style clashes with the student's style. If you are teaching your child yourself, you can easily remedy this by switching to materials more comfortable for him. If your child is being taught by someone else, often bringing your child's learning style to the teacher's attention will bring results. If, for some reason, the teacher will not accommodate your child's learning style, you can always try afterschooling— presenting the class information in the way your child learns best. He probably understood *some* of what he was exposed to in class, so this is not as much of a chore as you might expect, provided he is not totally discouraged.

You can help improve your learner's weak areas by simple exercises. The point here is not to teach him lots of new things during these exercises, but simply to practice other ways of learning until they become more comfortable. You can do visual memory exercises by showing your student a collection of items, then quickly covering it up and asking him to list the items. "Memory" games also provide fun and inexpensive visual practice. For auditory practice, list off strings of numbers or words and have him repeat them to you, or read him stories and have him narrate them back.

Our society does not generally stress tactile/kinesthetic learning, so your student may get great grades while remaining helpless in this area. That is one reason why so many people are unable to fix anything around their own homes. If you want to improve your child's tactile and kinesthetic skills, physical exercise of all sorts is good, as is practice in modeling with clay and making models from kits. Typing also develops tactile skills that are transferable to, say, piano playing, and it works the other way too.

The reason people avoid certain methods of learning is because those are uncomfortable for them. Have mercy when urging your children to use new channels. The idea is to stretch the learner just a little so he won't feel so uncomfortable next time.

THANK HEAVEN FOR LITTLE BOYS

Research has finally validated what mothers knew all along. In general, little boys are more physical, more aggressive, and less verbal than little girls. I say "in general" because some girls are tomboys (I was one) and some boys are naturally sedentary thinkers.

Today the average little boy desperately needs schoolproofing. The typical school environment rejects everything that is best about him. He wants to run and make noise. The school wants him to sit and be quiet. He wants to do active things. The school wants him to be passive. He is not particularly verbal. The school considers lack of immediate verbal ability a "disability" to be "remediated." No wonder little boys outnumber little girls more than two to one in "learning disabilities"![1]

In the old, bygone, sex-sterotyped days, little boys got to lord it over the girls (who had them beaten in the classroom) by playing rough games and doing the heavier classroom chores. If the girls, thanks to a one-year developmental head start, had taken over the Brains department, the boys could at least console themselves with their unquestioned ownership of the Muscle department.

But boys' games have been abolished. Tamed-down versions are now available with equal-sex participation. Everywhere judges are giving girls a boost, with rulings that require boys' teams to be open to girls but prevent boys from playing on girls' teams. Boys are legally prevented from ever showing superiority at anything.

The other refuge of budding manhood, tinkering with machines and wood, is now also sex-neutral. Little girls get Erector sets and tools for Christmas. (I did like my Erector set, too.)

So boys are blocked out from fulfilling their natural aggressiveness, and girls are encouraged to become more aggressive. Both are given the same career goals, with this one difference— that the more "manly" a boy is, the less likely he is to be able to reach any of the desired goals. The path to success is feminine: compliance with the teacher, quiet studiousness, verbal giftedness. Diplomas granted by mostly-female institutions have replaced hands-on ability as the measure of a man. And, in the hands of the kind of people who support Comparable Worth legislation, those diplomas would be even the final measure of a man's salary, as all the formulas for evaluating the "comparable worth" of jobs give virtually *no* points to the amount of physical effort, courage, or endurance necessary to the job.

All this would not matter much were it not that girls are much better as boys (under the new tamed-down rules) than boys are as girls. We don't secretly despair if our daughters fail to hit home runs each time they are at bat, but we do openly despair if our sons are slow to pick up reading skills.

I propose we stop acting ashamed of little boys, and energetic little girls. There's nothing wrong with lots of energy and a desire to be the boss. Give it a place to go instead of stomping on it. An example: We were looking at a house a while back. The owners, former foster parents, told us this story about two young fellows (call them John and Don) who came to live with them. The first two days, John and Don ran *everywhere.* Up the hill, down the hill, up the front steps, through the house, out the back, around the house. Nobody stopped them. The foster family was used to kids having strong reactions to a new placement. John and Don stopped running around wildly on the third day, and were subsequently enrolled in a local school.

Some time after this, the boys' caseworker came by to talk to the foster parents.

"Have you been giving John and Don their hyperactive medicine?" she inquired.

"Why, no," the foster mother replied. "Nobody told us they needed any medicine."

"Well, have you at least enrolled them in their Special Ed classes?"

"Special Ed? They're doing fine in regular classes!"

John and Don *needed* to run. They did not need counseling, Special Ed, or alligator tears of sympathy.

Running made them feel better. When they felt better, they acted better and started learning.

Another example: our friend Jim helped found a private school. I asked him if he had ever had any trouble with "hyperactive" children. "Oh, you mean those wired-up boys?" he grinned. "Nope, never had any trouble. Whenever one of them started jumping around and acting wild, I took him out to the football field and had him run around it a couple of times. Settled 'em right down."

Sweaty, hard work, whether running or some more obviously edifying pastime, deserves honor just as brain-work does. The child who finds the one difficult will almost invariably find success in the other. Why leave it to the street gangs to provide an environment where tough kids can find respect?

You can at least partially schoolproof your own tough little guy by showing your pride at his hands-on accomplishments. Workbook pages are not all there is to life. Any kid who can put together a racing car model or run a lathe has something going for him. So does a kid who will sweat and strain at a physical task without complaining. Encourage that something.

SPEED AND TIMING

In teaching, as in auto racing, timing is everything. The same car that, in the hands of one driver, flips out on the curve and bursts into flames, when steered by a gearshift jockey with better timing makes it victoriously around the curve and down the home stretch. Same car, but different use of brakes, acceleration, and steering.

People, similarly, learn at different rates. Not only that, people tend to learn in spurts. Instead of an even upward line on a chart, children typically learn in stairstep fashion . . .

moving along one level and then leaping to a new level of understanding. Thus, at any given time the nice even pace of our carefully crafted curriculum is bound to be boring one child silly while another is falling behind.

Simple solution: label the faster child "gifted" and the slower child "special" (it really means "stupid," as his little buddies will gleefully inform him). These labels work wondrously well. Later, when the "gifted" child starts falling behind in another subject (he's no longer on that learning spurt), we will insist he is still gifted and think we must not be motivating him. Meantime, we can discourage the "special" child so effectively that he won't even *try* to learn, making him even more "special."

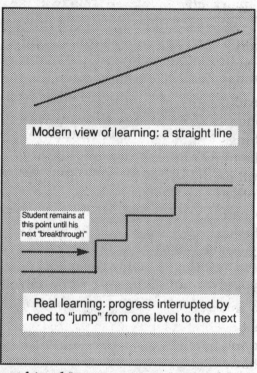

Modern view of learning: a straight line

Student remains at this point until his next "breakthrough"

Real learning: progress interrupted by need to "jump" from one level to the next

Maybe this simple solution isn't such a hot idea after all. How about an even simpler one: *fit the pace of learning to the individual child and don't worry about comparing him to others.* In theory, some of us believe in this. However, we have picked up the American feeling that everyone must be doing something every single minute. So we berate and push the temporarily sluggish student, making him (quite naturally) even more sluggish.

The simplest solution of all might be to simply *let kids alone every now and then.* If your learner doesn't get the idea, and doesn't get it, and continues to not get it, try giving it a rest. Do something else. Come back to the sticky area later, in a week or a month.

We have tried this with all of our children, and it really works. It also relieves a tremendous amount of strain on both parent (or teacher) and student.

Anxious as I am to introduce our children to the joy of reading, I have started them all on alphabet flash cards and phonics lessons at quite early ages. With both our older boys, things went swimmingly until we got to "blending"— putting the individual sounds together to make a word. In both cases I still hadn't verbalized the principle of giving things a rest, and only dropped my useless blending lessons when the boys became visibly frustrated. A few months later, in each case, the boys were blending just fine. Nothing magical happened except that they were a little older.

Little kids don't know enough to know what they don't know. In less mystical terms, they don't know what questions to ask to find the missing pieces. Perhaps a particular child is not even mature enough yet to understand the concept you are trying to teach, or perhaps he lacks some vital background that you have been assuming is there. In either case, it will work better to stop attacking the main subject and try feeling gently around the edges. If that, too, gets you nowhere, then a rest for both of you is in order.

Kids, of course, will try to sucker you into going easy on them. In this, they are exactly like adults. You will need to be able to distinguish between lateblooming, laziness, and deficiency.

- Lateblooming is when a child needs more time to learn.

- Laziness is when he won't even do what he knows how to do. (Very little kids forget things easily—keep this in mind).

- Deficiency is when the poor kid actually has something organic wrong with him. "Mental retardation" is not deficiency. It's what doctors say when they don't know what's wrong with you. On the other hand, identifiable birth defects may cause a child to be slower across the board than other children.

You need more patience for lateblooming and deficiency, less for laziness. Remembering that human beings are more than organic brain cells, I would be inclined to treat "deficient" kids as latebloomers who possess all the spiritual equipment of other human beings. This includes the ability to understand a story, make jokes, and resent being treated like a machine or animal.

If anything I've said so far contradicts your own experience, go ahead and ignore me. I'm not a card-carrying expert (thank goodness!) and therefore am not obligated to demand you ignore reality if it contradicts my prescriptions! Still, I think you'll find that a more mellow attitude towards the pace of learning— including the courage to forego teaching when it is obviously accomplishing nothing at the moment— will actually increase the speed at which your child learns.

MARKS-ISM vs. THE SCHOOL OF THE SECOND CHANCE

Behold the traditional method of grading. A student gets *one chance* at proving he has learned something. If he discovers he didn't learn it well enough the first time, grits his teeth, and finally learns it perfectly, does he get credit for his knowledge? No way! Often he is not allowed to take a test twice. In the cases where retesting is allowed, generally the two grades are averaged, or some similar scheme is employed to prevent the final mark reflecting what the student actually knows.

I used to think this was fair. That is because I was a fast learner and always did well on tests. If every Tom, Dick, and Harry were allowed to keep taking the test until he got it right (thus actually *learning* something), how would anyone know I was more wonderful than them? The dreaded scourge of Grade Inflation caused by all my classmates getting credit for learning the subject at a slower pace would devalue *my* A!

All I can say is that I was young and I wasn't a Christian. My father, a professor of philosophy, enlightened me on this topic one day. He asked me, "Mary, if you had a student who got an F on the first test in a course, a D on the second, a C on the third, a B on the fourth, and an A on the final, what grade would you give him?" After giving the matter deep thought and asked if the final was weighted more heavily than the other tests, I settled on a C grade. Dad then told me I was wrong. His reasoning, quite simply, was that he wanted to rate his students based on what they knew, and if a student had worked hard enough to pull himself up to an A understanding at last, he deserved an A.

We are assuming, of course, that grades have something to do with evaluating learning. However, schools today often use grades as a motivation device: a reward . . . or punishment. I call this "Marks-ism"— using grades to control people rather than to give them meaningful feedback that will help them target their future learning efforts. In some especially vile cases, teachers have even been known to fail children for poor attendance (whether they were sick or not), *regardless* of how they did on their homework and tests.[2]

The best you can do to schoolproof your children against the Marks-ists, if you leave your children in such a school (which I don't recommend), is to personally stress that YOU care about effort and progress, whatever the report card might say. Thus, a child who gets an A with no effort has accomplished nothing spiritually more significant than her sister who had to struggle for a C.

I would do my best also to wean children from the idea that a good grade is the ultimate goal of their studies. Sometimes he who studies harder and learns more gets a *worse* grade.

When I took my first college German course, I found myself in a very small class. It was the summer before school started, and only a few other people wanted to take German from 7:30 to 10:30 at night. The teacher, a strict Prussian sort, was determined not to be known as an easy grader. Thus, there would only be one A handed out in his section.

My main competition for that A was an older, married woman. She always wrote essays using only the vocabulary and grammatical forms we had studied so far. I, in contrast, constantly was trying out new words and new grammar, and naturally made more mistakes. I probably learned twice as much— but I only got a B.

Those of us who teach our own children, or run our own schools, are in a strong position to make our record-keeping and grading useful rather than destructive. For starters, we can determine to *throw away the steps and keep the results.* This is what we do in the real world. No businessman saves the first drafts of his memos. No homeworker treasures up her botched dress seams. Instead, the businessman tosses the first drafts as soon as he has the final copy in his hands, and the homeworker rips out the botched seam and replaces it with one sewn properly. As adults, we quite rightly want to be judged on our final products, not on our missteps along the way.

Children deserve the same respect.

This is not to imply that we should encourage slipshod work. You, as the teacher, will have to determine whether your students are really trying. Knowing human nature, though, children who know they will have to repeat a job until they get it right are unlikely to want to keep repeating it.

The difference between this and the behaviorist Mastery Learning approach, which doles out knowledge in small nibbles and *forbids* a child to tackle a higher step before conquering the lower, is that we can let our children play with knowledge at all levels and tackle, on their own initiative, whatever appeals to them, whether they are supposedly ready or not. We also can reserve the right to give one sticky spot a rest, or even choose to skip it entirely because it is in our judgment inessential to the real goal.

Humans are always capable of more than anyone expects. We must be just as careful to not hold our students back as not to push them further than they are ready. Let the little kids *try*, without labeling their trying with A's or F's, and then go from there.

IF YOU WANT A THING LEARNED RIGHT, LEARN IT YOURSELF

For some time I have been trying to figure out why everyone is so in love with homework. Homework always has seemed to me an imposition on the student and his family, and an admission that the school isn't capable of teaching the poor kid what he needs to know even in a six- or eight-hour day.

The other day I finally figured it out. Homework is something that the student does (ideally) *all on his own*. Kids are not encouraged to break into groups to do their homework.

Here we finally have a solitary (even if bored) mind tackling work on its own. Homework is a chance— the *only* chance many children get— to learn independent study habits.

My first objection still stands. Kids don't need to go home to practice independent study. Self-paced learning programs, in which children progress at their own rate through a predetermined course of study, provide all the benefits of homework without the homework. This is the way the famous universities, like Oxford and Cambridge, turned out thousands of matchless scholars.

A recent article in *World* magazine quoted a successful one-room-schoolhouse teacher as saying that the reason her students do so well is that they have learned to learn on their own. This was also given as an important reason for the relative academic success of private Christian schools, whose students test on the average a year or more ahead of public school students.

When I was in the sixth grade, I used to finish my seatwork early and settle down with a Tom Swift novel from the bookshelf at the back of the room. It was a good arrangement. Unfortunately, I had to prop the current Tom Swift adventure inside my textbook and pretend I was studying, as mere reading was not encouraged. But why not allow children who finish early to choose from a variety of quiet indoor activities (reading, painting, crafts) and noisy outdoor activities? To encourage the outdoor types, hire a full-time outdoor monitor. The teacher could then help slower students while the others looked after themselves. Those who finish gain independence. Those who need help gain extra attention.

Another wrinkle is to break kids into different groups for each subject. Thus, a girl could be in fourth-grade English, second-grade Math, third-grade History, and so on. This is the one-room-schoolhouse method. If provision is made for children who want to study extra hard and skip ahead in a given subject, it amounts to self-paced learning.

Children should not be penalized for legitimate differences in learning speed. Individualized self-paced learning accepts the differences; socialist whole-class teaching accents them.

God bless and keep the one-size-fits-all education crowd . . . far away from us!

PART IV

MAKING SCHOOL BEAUTIFUL

CHAPTER ELEVEN

MRS. FREEMAN'S ENRICHMENT PARK & EDUCATION EMPORIUM

Erma Bombeck once wrote a column in which she explained why mothers would never rise up and boycott the public school system, no matter how bad it got. The reason? American mothers have become dependent on the schools for baby-sitting their children. If the kids were home all day unexpectedly, according to Mrs. Bombeck, mothers would be forming lines outside the buildings begging the administrators to reopen.

Picture the tender scene:

"Hi, Mom. I'm home."

"Good golly! What are you doing here? It's only 10 AM!"

"Teacher's strike. They say it may last all week."

"Argh! They can't do this to me! I've got to find someplace to keep you all week?"

"I *could* stay home, Mom."

"Over my dead body! I've planned to do the spring cleaning."

When Erma Bombeck wrote her column, most mothers still were at home all day. Now that so many slave for wages outside the home, the tender scene becomes even more tender:

"Hi, Mom."

"Where are you calling from?"

"Jimmy's house. We're out of school."

"What are you doing out of school?"

"Teachers' strike. They say it may last all week."

"Argh! They can't do this to me! I've got to find someplace to keep you all week?"

"I *could* stay home, Mom."

"No way, kiddo. If I leave you alone all day I'll get hotlined for child neglect. And I'm sure not going to lose any work time and get in trouble with my boss staying home to babysit you."

Are most mothers as hard-boiled as the two in our scenes above? We can hope not. Still, when people get desperate they lose touch with the finer emotions. And many parents today would become desperate if suddenly forced to take care of their own children all by themselves.

Public schools are cashing in on this tremendous demand for baby-sitting services, which they have also actively worked to create. "Family Life" courses, for example, invariably contain some propaganda to the effect that children develop much better when separated from their families as soon after birth as possible and placed in institutional educational facilities. Meanwhile, the NEA pushes for ever-earlier compulsory schooling and ever-longer school days and school years.

If the public schools ever admitted that they were simply trying to become the nation's baby-sitter, they would lose the leverage afforded by compulsory school attendance laws. Call baby-sitting of three-year-olds "Early Childhood Education" and you can convince people that this "education" is vital to children's success in life, and that therefore every child should be forced into it. Educators also get paid more than baby-sitters, a fact of which the NEA is well aware.

All of this bodes ill for true education. If kids are going to be warehoused in school buildings from 7 AM to 7 PM so their parents can pursue careers without inconvenience— and if the kids in those buildings have to be hectored from morning to night with structured programs and activities, plus homework for when they finally do arrive home— when are these kids ever going to find the time to be kids? To think? To play? We're looking at the return of forced child labor. Twelve hours a day plus overtime. All so the grownups can kid themselves that they are warehousing the kids "for their own good."

An obvious way to sidestep this situation is to stay home and home school your children. Another is to place them in a private school with a reasonably short school day. Private schools, though, are under the same pressures to provide baby-sitting as the public schools. Parents have to be able to drop children off and pick them up at hours possible for them. And private schools, too, tend to fill up the extra hours children stay after school with structured programs and activities— plus those much-in-demand homework assignments for the evening hours at home.

Is there any way we can take the pressure off our kids? Does all education outside the home have to take so *long* . . . and leave so little free time? Are kids in school doomed forever to one-grade-fits-all education, in which they can only move with their class at the class's speed? Is the model of classroom-and-teacher something that came down from the clouds over Mount Sinai, or are there more flexible alternatives? Or can private schools, especially Christian private schools, become really different than public schools— more human and more beautiful?

MRS. FREEMAN'S ENRICHMENT PARK

Private schools can make a giant stride forward by recognizing they perform two functions, education and baby-sitting, and that the two should not be mixed. Charlotte Mason's Parent's National Education Union schools, for example, gave lessons in the morning and let the children play freely outdoors in the afternoon. Thus, the children were taught, and those who needed to remain at school after their lessons were over were not denied free time. School was school in the morning and "home" in the afternoon— a place where children could play as they do at home, without someone standing over them every minute and telling them how to play. Their free time was enriching; they weren't just warehoused. Later on in this chapter we'll explore just how free time can be made enriching without stifling children's freedom.

. . . AND EDUCATION EMPORIUM

Why, when Christian schools were started as a distinctly biblical endeavor, do so many follow the public school model of one-age-one-grade classes? Is there any biblical reason why first-graders must take all first grade courses? Would the world come to an end if some second-graders were in first-grade math, and some first-graders were in third-grade English?

An Education Emporium is a place where you go to buy just exactly the education you want. You sign up, for example, for Phonics 2 and Math 2 and Guitar 1 and History 3. If the private schools became education emporiums instead of public school copies, children could take the courses they need without any funny business about "staying back a grade" or being labeled Slow or Gifted. A faster child could study on his own and skip ahead to more advanced classes. Slower children could take difficult courses twice. (I would suggest that courses last no more than three months and be broken up into smaller segments, each offered more than once a year, so students won't be forced to repeat an entire year if they fall behind in one segment.)

"But this could never work!" Oh yes it could! In fact, you yourself have seen it working at your neighborhood community college. Students sign up for the courses they want. Some courses have prerequisites, others don't. Some are core courses and others are optional. If a student flunks a course, he can usually take it over the next semester. If he has free time between classes, he can study, do homework, flop on the grass, or whatever he wishes.

Here are some of the advantages of the Education Emporium approach:

1. **No need for endless review** in every grade of subjects and skills supposedly already learned. Right now private schools and public schools alike feel compelled to start every semester of every subject practically back in kindergarten, since attaining a certain grade level is no proof a child knows anything at all. This is a tremendous waste of time, and discouraging to the children who *have* already learned the material. The total learning program could be condensed at least 50 percent by just eliminating this excessive reviewing.

2. **Children are treated as individuals,** and rewarded according to their progress, with the reward being the privilege of doing more advanced work.

3. **Learning on one's own**—a Christian virtue—is encouraged, since you can skip ahead in a particular subject by doing this and testing out of a level.

4. **Slower students don't need to miss a whole year of progress in all subjects and be labeled as well.** Each class would contain a mix of ages based solely on the children's ability to do the work.

5. **Educational failure would be virtually nonexistent.** You simply go back to the level you haven't mastered and proceed from there. A thirteen-year-old who can't read would take Phonics 1 and 2. He would then be encouraged to study on his own and leapfrog up the English ladder until he arrived at his own age group. Since older children learn more quickly when they do learn, this is what would happen in the vast majority of cases.

6. **Students would benefit from social interaction with a wider range of people** than the age-segregated peer group.

7. **Children and their parents are no longer passive patients of education,** but actively involved in crafting the child's education.

8. **Teaching is much easier.** Teachers can count on a class of students all ready and able to learn the material. In other words, teachers will be able to *teach,* rather than constantly having to review and remediate.

The only real problem with setting up an education emporium is scheduling. This is a bit tougher than for the one-grade-fits-all format, though not that much tougher. A suggestion: schedule all course levels to meet at the same time (e.g., English 1, 2, 3, etc.); schedule all core classes for the morning and electives in the afternoon. You won't need all day for the core subjects if you eliminate educational clutter (see

Chapter 8). If high schools can schedule for diverse educational paths, so can you.

CRUISING THE EDUCATION EMPORIUM

While we're talking about educational emporiums, we might as well have some fun and imagine what one might look like. Take Mrs. Freeman's Enrichment Park and Education Emporium. Dear old Mrs. Freeman's children are all grown and her husband is with the Lord. So she decided to start an academy based on her best ideas of what Christian schooling should be.

The "enrichment park" part of the Freeman enterprise refers to the fact that *children can stay for as much or as little of the day as their parents desire.* Home schoolers can drop off their children for a phonics or art class without having to sign up for a full program. If the parents can't get back to pick up the children right after class is out, the children can play on the playground, read in the library, or mess about in the Free Art area. Similarly, children can stay after regular classes are finished, waiting for their moms to come by after work and pick them up.

In Mrs. Freeman's Education Emporium, you get what you pay for. Every class counts separately on your bill. Some families sign up for just the core subjects; others add enrichment subjects; home schoolers, as we mentioned, may sign up for just one subject.

Age is no barrier to enrollment in a class. In fact, every student coming into Mrs. Freeman's school is evaluated for competency in every subject area and placed in a class at that level, regardless of his or her age.

Some subjects have prerequisites. *Prerequisites can be waived if the student has learned the material on his own.* The prerequisite for Phonics 1 is a Stories course, where the teacher reads aloud from a variety of interesting literature. If a student has been read to a lot at home, the Stories course can be waived. Similarly, Premath (counting and using manipulatives) is a prerequisite to Math 1, and World History Outlined is a prerequisite for all other history courses.

Because older children and even some adults can be found at many class levels, Mrs. Freeman's teachers *avoid the use of cutesy twaddle* in their classes. Because younger children can be found at many class levels, the teaching in those courses has become *more entertaining*. Because of the age mixing, and because your real achievement consists of progress rather than making a better grade than others in your class, there is *a more cooperative class spirit*.

Oh, I forgot to mention— at Mrs. Freeman's you either *do it right or do it over*. Thus, everyone eventually gets an A. Students are encouraged to help each other succeed. You never lose status because someone else succeeds.

EARLY CHILDHOOD AGGRAVATION

Where do preschoolers and babies come into Mrs. Freeman's setup? Ideally, they don't. Education is not baby-sitting, and very little children are not ready for formal education. For little children, formal Early Childhood Education is not a bonanza but an aggravation.

The facts of the case are this:

1. Little children prefer their own homes and families.

2. Little kids don't learn at the same rate as older children. You have to repeat an idea or fact ten times as often to a two-year-old as a four-year-old, and ten times as often to a four-year-old as an eight-year-old.

3. Little children lack certain skills you can take for granted with older children (such as potty training and adult-style logic).

Why don't babies and preschoolers belong in school? The obvious first answer is that God designed babies to be brought up in their own families.

BABY LIBERATION

My baby Franky is crawling about the floor. I just spent an hour talking with his father while we both watched him. Up to the bookcase reaching for a book. On the floor playing with the book. The book starts to feel the strain of a baby's attention, so we gently remove it and remind Franky, "You must be *gentle* with books. Turn the pages like this." Now over to the toy box. He has a piece of tissue paper in his hand and is starting to chew it. I remove the tissue paper quickly before he tries to swallow it. Up onto Mommy's lap, reaching for my papers. I hold him back and cuddle him. He pokes at my face, first carefully and then more vigorously. Bill reminds Franky to be gentle with Mommy. He cries at the reprimand. I hug him. Over to Daddy. Daddy swoops Franky into the air, getting a tremendous giggle out of him. Do it again! And again! Back to the books . . .

You can't give a baby any amount of freedom unless someone is free to watch him. And you can only watch a few free-roaming babies at once. That's why day-care centers stack babies in cribs in front of television sets. That's also why anything calling itself Education for Babies is doomed to become a variation on the life-in-the-playpen theme.

Babies need a tremendous amount of attention. Diapers. Bottles. Cuddling. It costs a fortune to pay an outsider to provide all that.

That's why Mrs. Freeman's emporium should *not* get involved in Baby Education. Baby care can only be good if it is a ministry. You can never afford to pay what it is worth.

This is also why the suggestion that one bunch of mothers watch another bunch's children so the first bunch can afford to stay home makes no sense. If you already have two children of your own to watch, the last thing you need is four more preschoolers from four more families. Even so, the most you could expect to make (before expenses) from this chaos on wheels is about $8,000 a year. *None* of the children will be getting the attention he needs, and you're not making any serious money anyway.

In cultures that are less anti-child, nobody gets paid for baby-sitting. People consider children to be treasures and are glad to serve them. Looking upon babies as income or expenses prevents us from seeing them as human beings made in the image of God.

Babies need to explore freely, within limits, and learn to obey the rules. This they can and should learn at home. If neither of two parents wants to stay home with the baby, the least they should do is provide their baby with freedom in someone else's home, or provide a nanny or housekeeper for their own home. In the case where a single parent really needs help with the baby, would it be too much to ask older women in the church— who are supposed to help and teach the younger women— to look after the baby as a ministry?

PRESCHOOL LIBERATION

Young children enjoy and need

- Art and crafts experience (handling small real-world objects and making pretty and useful things with them).

- Stories read to them or told to them.
- Lots of real-world experiences in the company of their families (visiting the supermarket, library, Post Office, park . . .).
- Access to interesting material, some of which counts as "educational" (animals, globes, books, cultural artefacts . . .).
- Lots of time outdoors.
- Lots of time with their parents.

This meshes well with what the Bible says about people in general and children in particular. Since God is the Creator and we are made in His image, part of being human is being creative— making lovely things. Thus, the arts and crafts. Similarly, God is the great Storyteller. Much of the Bible is in the form of stories. Furthermore, parents and grandparents are specifically commanded to share God's stories with their children and grandchildren (Psalm 78). Thus, the importance of stories to a young child. God wants us to be "in the world, not of it." So segregating children from the world by confining them to a special "children's environment" is the exact opposite of preparing them for it. Again, part of the world is access to real and interesting materials and God's outdoor creation. This is all part of the much-talked-about but little-understood Christian worldview. On top of this all, to understand and relate to God as a Father, children absolutely need to develop strong, unchallenged attachments to their own parents.

A good preschool can provide much of the above. However, this properly counts as pre-education more than education with a capital E. Plus, you have some of the same problems with finding enough qualified teachers for the pittance the parents are likely to pay. Double plus, the kids don't really want to be there, and *somebody* ought to pay some attention to what they want. Triple plus, the preschool program is totally different from the regular school-age program, and can't be integrated into it. Eight-year-olds can learn with seven-year-olds or ten-year-olds, but three-year-olds can't. They need extra repetition, simpler explanations, and lots of time spent teaching or practicing really basic skills, like potty training and how to hold the scissors.

Your home, in contrast, can provide *everything* your preschool child needs, and do it better than the preschool. Take your little one with you in your normal daily rounds and he'll have far more real-world experiences than the formally preschooled set. Arts and crafts? Almost all your household trash can be turned into art projects. Outdoor play time? No problem. Time with you? No problem. Having books read to him? No problem.

But you can go farther than a preschool should. You can give him a chance at formal education *without* the pressure of a formal program. You see, a formal in school phonics program *has* to pressure the kids to achieve, because the parents are paying for the kids to learn phonics. But nobody is paying *you* to teach your four-year-old to read, so if he doesn't get it right away or isn't interested yet it's no big deal. Again, a formal Early Childhood Education program has to concentrate on forcing children to conform in large groups, to sit nicely at their little desks and work on their little worksheets, to stand in line and wash their hands, and so on. You don't have to control a large group of preschoolers, so you can let your child find his own pace. You can afford to try more educational adventures without risking anything.

HEARD ANY GOOD YOKES LATELY?

"It is good for a man to bear the yoke when he is young" (Lamentations 3:27). Some have taken this verse and run with it. They say that God must mean for very little children to submit to formal, structured, we-tell-you-what-you-do-next learning. Otherwise the children will grow up to be self-centered humanists.

Ah, the joys of unconditional obedience! Neat little rows of children all ready to do exactly what you say. Surely this must be Christian! After all, God insists that we obey Him with perfect obedience. Wouldn't the best way to learn this obedience be to follow arbitrary classroom rules?

The context of this verse talks about seeking the Lord and waiting patiently for Him to save us. It has nothing whatsoever to say about recommending institutional settings for young children. The "yoke" referred to is the spiritual yoke of submission to God— the same yoke Jesus meant when He said that His yoke was easy and His burden was light.

The problem with training kids to render total, automatic obedience to an authority figure is that there are lots of bad authority figures out there. Think for instance of Hitler and Stalin, both the legal leaders of their countries. Now imagine the Gestapo, who after all are the duly appointed representatives of the legal Nazi government, knocking on your door. "Tell us who in your neighborhood is hiding Jews. We want to take them to the concentration camp and gas them to death." "Oh, kind sirs, we cannot refuse anything to the duly appointed authorities of our people. The Millers down the street have two Jews in their attic."

The difficult task of Christian training is to raise kids who are more obedient to God than they are to us. The task of Christian training is *not* to raise children who have learned to conform without question to a totally artificial classroom model.

What do we want for our children? Do we want little robots raised by surrogate mothers, robots who aren't even allowed to prefer staying home because that is "rebelling against the yoke"? Or do we want happy, wise, spiritually alive kids who know alternatives and how to choose between them? Are we interested in giving our kids freedom and responsibility, or just in controlling them so they won't bother us?

Responsibility can't be learned in the absence of freedom. And we Christians, of all people, need to fear freedom the least. "Where the Spirit of the Lord is, there is freedom." If our God really is a Rock, we can afford to put our weight on the Rock. Our children will never know how solid God is unless they have a chance for free time, for thinking, for experiencing God's creation without some well-meaning adult telling them every second what to think about it.

There are yokes, and there are yokes. "It is for freedom that Christ has set us free. Stand firm, then, and do not let yourselves be burdened again by a yoke of slavery" (Galatians 5:1).

THE SOUL RESULT OF REAL EDUCATION

What can we expect from children educated as significant human beings and allowed as much freedom as they show they are responsible to handle?

First, they will be more solid in their beliefs. They will know how to gather facts and make informed choices. They will have tasted the joys of both freedom and responsibility.

Second, such children will not be easy to brainwash or manipulate.

Third, they will be less anxious. Coming from the solid base of the home (or at least a homelike) environment where children are treasured, not measured, they will be able to concentrate more on reaching their goals and less on maintaining an image or impressing others.

"But what will they *know?*" Good question. Let's now see what the possibilities are for truly Christian curriculum content and design.

CHAPTER TWELVE

GODLINESS WITH CONTENT

You are in a plane. The day is clear, with a brilliant blue cloudless sky. Looking down, you see the world spread out beneath like a multicolored carpet. Green fields dot the landscape, separated by ribbons of road. Small towns spread like matchbox cities; rivers run like glowing threads. As night falls, you look down on the twinkling lights of cities and dark patches of forest.

What did you see? You saw the world— at least the part of it your plane flew over! You saw *all* of it, as planes are not equipped with blinders to prevent passengers from looking at unauthorized areas. You saw it as a whole, yet made up of parts: farms, towns, woods, cities, rivers, lakes, roads, shopping malls.

Education should give your child an "eye on the world." Through his education, he can learn what is in the world, how the parts are connected, what they mean, and what he should do with his life in this world.

But will he get a chance to learn all this?

CONTENT IN THE HANDS OF AN ANGRY MOB

We all know what the standard curriculum is supposed to cover: math, language arts, science, social studies (not history or geography, mind you), physical education, art (possibly), music (possibly), and, if you attend public school, a spattering of other "educations" like drug education and nuclear education. Now, the question. Where did this outline come from? A sudden flash of insight? A mountaintop revelation– "Thou Shalt Require Social Studies"?

The reasons offered for current curriculum content vary from "teaching children to fit into society" (Robot Education) to "helping them get a good job" (Employed Robot Education). Now and then an old, gray-haired humanist will be heard muttering about the need for a common culture, but you can be sure neither Christian nor public schools ever listen to people like that. He wouldn't be able to explain what he means by a "common culture" anyway, at least to the satisfaction of his fellow feminist and Black Power humanists.

Modern curriculum is utilitarian. "We do it because it gets results." (Never mind *what* results!) Since curriculum control is power, special interest groups insist the curriculum must reflect their agenda and contain their authors. Even while the schools were being integrated, curriculum was becoming segregated. Theoretically, now black kids need their own history, literature, art, and music classes, as do Hispanics, Orientals, feminists, and homosexuals.[1] The rest of the curriculum becomes technicalities without soul. Art appreciation as a list of artists to memorize. Famous Politicians of the Twentieth Century. Lists, lists, lists, all without inner meaning.

Oh, yes, children are also taught "thinking skills" as a sop to the humanists. Ignoring the fact that children are *born* with thinking skills, educational humanists bravely press on, trying to teach children to be what they already are— human.

And that is current educational content at its *best*. In reality, even this sorry content is lost in favor of playing psychological games with schoolchildren.

CHRISTIAN EDUCATION TODAY

Christian education claims a different starting-point— the Bible— and a different authority— God. Still, Christian education too often is a clone of the public school agenda, plus an added-on Bible course. The same applies to individual subjects, which more often than not rigorously follow the public school schedule. We sanitize the public school courses, add some Christian history and word problems back in, and mix in devotions. Thus, the current Christian curriculum has far more in common with the current counter-Christian curriculum than it does with Christian education of the past.

But should devotions be the *only* real difference between Christian education and counter-Christian education? Is even adding moral and historical content to the secular agenda enough to make it uniquely Christian?

Christian education won't be Christian until we let the Bible, not bureaucrats, determine its content. In fact, no brand of education can be true to itself until its designers face up to this very important question of content. *What* will our children study? And *why?* There can be no more important educational question than this.

A DISCLAIMER

Before we go any farther, I would like to make it clear that I do *not* believe in forcing people to adopt any one educational system, including the one I am about to suggest. All I can do is share the best of my own thinking, which itself has in large part been gleaned from the best of others'.

If you are a fellow Christian, we can appeal to the same Authority. Thus you and I both have the right to present our best biblical case to one another in hopes of edifying one another.

If you are not a Christian, all I ask is this: check out these ideas by God's Word and by your own experience of reality. If I miss the mark biblically, that's my fault, not the Bible's. But if what the Bible says makes sense, perhaps you could reconsider your current spiritual position. Truth is truth, after all, even if it bothers Norman Lear and Phil Donahue!

TOOLS TO LOVE AND SERVE GOD
AND OUR NEIGHBOR

Let's imagine our dream curriculum. What would the ultimate Christian curriculum look like?

Remember that verse in Timothy: "The goal of this command is love . . . " (1 Timothy 1:5). Love of whom? Of God and our neighbor, as Jesus said these were the two greatest commandments, from which all the others flowed and on which they depended.

The goal of Christian education should be to give people the tools to love and serve God and their neighbor.

Now, what are those tools?

KNOWING GOD

You can't love and serve a person you don't know. So the Christian curriculum starts with introducing students to God.

Knowing God is more than knowing facts about God. It requires, as Susan Schaeffer Macaulay so beautifully puts it, "a sense of wondering, questioning, awe."[2] So from the start our entire curriculum must treat our students as human beings rather than as empty buckets to fill with knowledge or unruly animals to train. We must give them the soul and story along with the outer husk of facts.

How?

By becoming "as little children" ourselves (Matthew 18:3). We ourselves must share our wonder, our questions, our awe with our children.

If we are too stodgy to notice and delight in the sunshine of a spring day, or too proud to openly admit our failures, children will learn that our talk of God is word games. What *really* counts with us are phony social rules. If, in contrast, we dare to be *alive*— to show wonder in a blasé age and awe in a brazen generation— our students will see that we truly do worship a God who transcends social fads. If, on top of this, we dare to allow honest questions, we show that we really believe in a God who has answers. Nothing so reveals a practical atheist in Christian's clothing as his unwillingness to give God a chance to answer the questions he himself can't yet answer.

Bible

The Bible is the rock and foundation of a Christian curriculum. It is the way we learn about God, ourselves, our neighbors, and the world. This Book *explains* things. It tells us why they are what they are and what it all means. It even explains the future!

That being so, it seems only fair to let the Bible actually speak for itself. The first duty of a Christian curriculum is to get students intimate with what the Bible says. They need to know Bible history— by reading it through. They need to know the Bible's teaching on all sorts of subjects— by reading it through. What they do not need is little snippets taught topically and out of context, so they have no way of checking what they are taught to see if it's accurate.

Here the Christian curriculum often needs a lot of reform. Don't we commonly use Bible stories instead of the Bible itself to program (excuse me, I meant "teach") the little kids? And when they get a bit older, don't we tell them every second what lesson they are supposed to be learning from the Bible passage, instead of letting it speak to them? Don't we clutter up their time with endless activities based on the moral-of-the-week, so even if they discern more in the passage than we are ready for them to see we can easily distract them back to *our* agenda? Can anyone explain to me why the goal of first-grade Bible curriculum (and I've seen *lots* of Bible curriculum) typically is "developing self-esteem" rather than knowing what the Bible *says* about anything?

Prayer

Prayer is the language arts of dealing with God. It has two parts: how to speak (what kind of things God wants us to tell Him and ask Him) and how to listen (meditation).

Christian meditation is sorely neglected these days. We seem to have the idea that God *will* hear us because of our "much speaking," Jesus' words to the contrary.

I would like to suggest some simple ideas for a curriculum of prayer:

1. Taking the time to research your prayer requests, to know what you are asking for and what, if anything, you can do about them, keeps prayer from becoming a frustrating whining session.

2. "God is in heaven and you are on earth. Therefore let the

words of your mouth be few" (Ecclesiastes 5:2). It is also most worthwhile to think prayerfully through what you are asking, to see if it jibes with God's Word or not, before you start asking it.

3. Listening to God: according to the Bible, if you want to hear God's voice in your heart, you need to meditate on His Word. This means thinking over such Scriptures as come to mind and puzzling over them with an "open ear." It also means turning first to the Bible when you have a problem to see what answers you can find.

4. Prayer is sometimes broken down into Adoration, Confession, Thanksgiving, and Supplication. The sensitive soul will confess and supplicate automatically as need arises. Adoration and thanksgiving are meant to be an ongoing heart attitude. God hates phony posturing: thus the idea that every prayer should include confession, adoration, thanksgiving, and supplication regardless of the prayer's feelings at the time is asking for trouble. Look at the Psalms! Are these four-part business letter-type prayers (salutation, confession, problems, closing praise)? In reality, God sends the troubled soul the peace to adore and give thanks when these are initially the farthest things from his experience. Kids shouldn't be asked to fake spiritual rapture when they ought to be confessing spiritual deadness and begging for help.

As far as I can see, the command to "pray always" does not mean to spend your whole life talking at God. It means to spend your whole life *listening* to God, and that we should say to him the prayers He gives us (in Christian jargon, "burdens us" with). If we listened to Him more, instead of telling Him what we want to do and practically ordering Him to bless us, Western civilization wouldn't be in its present state.

Logic

Anyone who reads and understands the Bible, especially the Epistles, will understand logic. He may not know the technical terms involved, but he will know how to wield the spiritual sword without cutting off his own hands. Never underestimate the power of biblical teaching in the hands of someone who knows how to present and defend it!

Morals (God's Law)

Morals— how we should treat our neighbor— did not just bounce out into the world one day, as Athena supposedly sprang full-grown from the brow of Zeus. Neither did cobwebbed wise men ponder them into existence. They are all right there in the Ten Commandments and the other biblical rules that give applications of those commandments. Happily, the Ten Commandments are easy to memorize, especially in condensed form, as below:

1. No other gods.
2. No idols.
3. Don't take God's name in vain.
4. Keep God's Day holy.
5. Honor your father and mother.
6. No murdering.
7. No sex outside legitimate marriage.
8. No stealing.
9. No slander.
10. No coveting what isn't yours.

It may take an eternity to fully comprehend the noble breadth of these commands, but any two-year-old can understand them enough to at least begin obeying them.

Self (God-Esteem)

Plato said, "Know thyself." Today we have the notion that we can know ourselves by asking ourselves what we think of ourselves. We call this "self-esteem" and go to great lengths to foster kind thoughts about ourselves.

According to the Bible, we will never really get to know ourselves this way. To know yourself, you need to know what *God* thinks of you. This means letting the Word of God probe you and (quite often) find you wanting. Your job then is to improve and be found less wanting the next time.

How much does God think you and I are worth? Jesus said we are "worth more than many sparrows"— not exactly an encouragement to consider ourselves Masters of the Universe. Those who reject God and His laws are termed "worthless." "The wicked are like chaff, which the wind drives away" (Psalm 1).

Jesus did not die on the Cross because we are worth so much. He died on the Cross to *make* us worth something. Those who recognize their worthlessness and believe that Christ's sacrifice paid the price to wipe out their sins and give them a new life become children of God. Those who stubbornly cling to their own worth and their own ways remain outside the circle of God's esteem. This is the gospel as it was preached for twenty centuries, before the non-Christian Abraham Maslow "discovered" we need self-esteem more than we need God-esteem.

Take a look at the old *McGuffey Readers,* or other nineteenth-century readers influenced by Christianity, and you will see how far we have fallen. Children in those stories were warned not to take bad roads or to fall in with bad companions, lest they become worthless. Conversely, children who acted nobly were commended. Now we can't bear to admit that anyone ever really does wrong as a matter of choice, and our kids, regardless of their spiritual position, go about loudly singing, "Jesus loves me, this I know."

I strongly suggest that we heave all the self-esteem rubbish right out of our curriculum and get back to God's objective standards for judging ourselves— before He has to step in and show us the awful truth against our wills.

KNOWING AND SERVING OUR NEIGHBOR

Christians of times past used to talk about learning to become "useful." They thought that loving one's neighbor meant more than having warm fuzzies or even donating to Band Aid. God wanted us to first know our neighbor, then put our skills to use serving our neighbor.

What does it mean to know and serve your neighbor?

First, it means developing a worldview. I have carefully avoided using the term "worldview" so far, because I thought it would be a good idea to define it before talking about it. A worldview most literally would mean something like your view from the plane ride at the beginning of the chapter. You see what is there and how it relates to the rest of what's there. Informed by the Bible, you also see what it means and what, if anything, you should do about it. This is the basic knowledge human beings need in this world.

Second, you have to develop skills. Babies are good at crawling and babbling, but you can't help people much by crawling and babbling. Developing basic skills is stewardship of our minds and bodies.

Third, you have to discover and fit yourself for your particular calling. A calling is your mission from God to the world. Unlike the secular idea of job or career, a calling is not primarily a means to money and prestige. It may be unpaid, as the work of a mother at home. You may even have to pay for the privilege of following your calling— funding it perhaps with a job or savings from a job. You follow your calling for love: love of God and your neighbor. This calling is most usually not full-time Christian service. It is, however, full-time *cultural* service. Art, architecture, engineering, plumbing, farming, writing, medical work, law, car mechanics, and so on can all be callings. This is the work *you* are best suited to do in order to bless the world.

Fourth, you have to fit yourself for your role as a man or woman who may become a mother or father. Your children will be little "neighbors" who you will have to love and serve, and they will appreciate the time you spent preparing to greet them!

BASIC WORLDVIEW

Look up "aardvark" in an encyclopedia. You will find an entry that tells you more or less about aardvarks, but nothing about what people who live with aardvarks think of aardvarks. Even less will you discover God's view of or plan for the aardvark. You get facts, but no worldview.

After thinking for a long time about how we should organize basic knowledge to present it to learners, I would like to share with you what appear to be the best two organizing principles: history and geography.

Organizing Your Worldview with Geography

The best way to understand a real worldview is to literally look over the world. Do you know what the people in India believe, how they live, what art they have and why they developed that particular form of art, their political structure and how they treat their neighbors, what animals and plants live in India and how people live with them? If you don't know these things, your worldview is missing India. Geographically, you can easily see what countries you know enough to have a view of and which you don't.

The plain fact is that, as much as we talk about developing a Christian worldview, we are woefully deficient in our knowledge about the rest of the world. Americans hardly know anything about Canada. Canadians hardly know anything about Mexico. Mexicans hardly know anything about England. And so on.

I am not talking about giving students bits and pieces from around the world. What we should aim for here is real understanding of how people live and think in these countries, informed by our prior understanding according to the Bible of how people ought to live and think.

We look around the world and try to see other people as they see themselves and as God sees them. We look at their geography, their climate, their houses, their customs, their arts and politics. We look at their plants and animals. None of these facts are isolated from each other in real life! Furthermore, this is a much more interesting and systematic way to learn about the world.

Thus, the aardvark is not studied in isolation as a "fact," but in terms of what the people who live with aardvarks think and do about them, and how the other animals and plants that live near aardvarks are affected by aardvarks. The aardvark is also looked at with a sense of wonder in terms of his special purpose in God's creation. Science data is integrated into the real world once again.

In this age where Christians are commanded to disciple all nations, we really ought to have some idea what the rest of the world is like.

Organizing Your Worldview with History

The other perfectly natural way to organize your worldview is according to its history. The Bible itself starts off with a history of the ancient world, and continues this historical approach right into the New Testament and through the Book of Revelation at the end.

History is much more than what we normally think of as history: American History, European History, World History. Each culture has its own history, which should be at least glanced at as we progress geographically through the cultures of the world. Each discipline also has its own history: theology, art, music, science, engineering, cookery, and education, to name just a few.

Giving children just the modern view of things amounts to censorship. As some ancient author said, "To have no knowledge of history is forever to remain a child." We need the past as a measuring rule by which to compare the present. Since so much of Western civilization's past was Christian, and so much of its present is emphatically not Christian, we all the more need the perspective of the past.

Tracing a discipline from its roots to the present also teaches us how men discover and solve problems in that discipline. Thus the student becomes a co-discoverer with the greats of the past.

BASIC SKILLS (CLOSED SYSTEM)

We may not always agree on what skills are basic, but I am going to make a stab at listing some possibilities. Note that these all are "closed system" skills: once you have learned the skill, you have it. Therefore we should plan to teach these skills and put them into practice, rather than crafting our curriculum to keep on teaching these skills forever.

Phonics

Absolutely basic. Theoretically you can give your learner a complete worldview simply by telling him stories and showing him pictures; but if you want him to learn anything on his own, the sooner he is reading, the better.

Handwriting and Typing

Typing may not be considered a basic skill, although it is actually easier than handwriting. However, everyone needs one or both of these to function effectively today.

Grammar

Formal grammar study is not basic. What is basic is knowing the right type of word to use and the right type of punctuation. This, again, is a matter of limited study, since grammar is fixed.

Ciphering

Otherwise known as Arithmetic. The Bible presupposes its readers know how to count, add, subtract, multiply, divide, and use fractions, time, and measurement. Again, these skills are not complicated.

Drawing

A method of communication at least as powerful as writing, drawing is usually neglected as a basic skill. Yet more people have been artists throughout history than have been scribes. Simple line drawing is easy to learn— why not teach it?

Crafts

Not everyone will be interested in the same crafts. However, the same principles apply to every craft: design, following instructions, careful work, cleaning up your messes.

Household Skills—Cooking, Cleaning . . .

Do you want a child around the house who doesn't know how to clean up after himself? And wouldn't it be nice if they knew how to prepare at least simple foods for themselves? Can you picture a teenager who doesn't know how to make himself a ham sandwich? Case closed.

Teaching

Like cooking and cleaning, teaching can become a calling. However, the basic principles of how to teach can and should be learned by everyone. See Chapter 3.

Argumentation

A really basic skill. Babies are born ready to argue. You just need to teach them the rules (use logic, no fair hitting or breaking things if you lose).

Scientific Method

Takes less than an hour to teach. Establish the problem. Form a hypothesis. Develop a test. Design the test so your hypothesis has a chance to fail as well as to succeed. Other people must also be able to duplicate your test results. Use your hypothesis to predict outcomes. If the hypothesis good at predicting outcomes and passes a lot of different tests, it gets to be a theory. Theories are not infallible: see the history of science. Scientists are not infallible; see the history of theories.

TECHNICAL SKILLS (SPECIALIZED OR OPEN-ENDED)

These are all optional, since they are matters of one's individual calling. Technical skills include: • higher math • engineering • physics and other advanced sciences • animal husbandry • engine mechanics • and so on.

MOTHERING AND FATHERING

Like basic household skills and social skills, training in mothering and fathering is meant to happen in the home. The Church helps out in these areas by selecting qualified older men and women to train the younger men and women (see Titus 2:3-8, for example).

SCHOOLPROOFING YOUR CHILD, OR WHAT DAD TAUGHT ME ON MY SUMMER VACATION

The wonderful thing about the curriculum outlined above is that you can do it all yourself if need be.

Want to develop your child's sense of awe? Just be yourself, a childlike Christian, as you sit down, rise up, and walk with your children in the way (Deuteronomy 6:7).

Need to develop your learner's knowledge of the Bible and prayer life? Try family worship and church services.

Learning to read is easy. My *NEW Big Book of Home Learning* lists over a dozen good phonics programs designed for use in the home or school.

Want to teach basic skills? Again, the *NEW Big Book* and its companion volume, *The Next Book of Home Learning*, list hundreds of sources for instruction in every basic skill.

Teaching skills? You've got them now, if you carefully read this book!

Argumentation and logic? Study the Bible.

Worldview is a bit more difficult. You first have to develop your own worldview, then share it with your learner. Materials for this are not readily available at the moment, although you can scrape together quite a curriculum with just the public library and handouts from missionary organizations. I see a real need for publishers to develop materials that present an integrated Christian worldview and for schools to develop courses to teach this.

Technical skills are much more available than worldview instruction. Some sources where you can learn technical skills: libraries, correspondence schools, apprenticeships, and universities. Of these, my opinion is that the universities are the least efficient and most corrupt means of gaining this knowledge.

We have covered a lot of ground in this book. We have looked at the *purpose* of education . . . the *methods* of education . . . and which techniques legitimately serve a proper purpose and method. We have just finished trying to organize the *content* of education, so we can see if our children are actually getting this content or not. We have also examined the *structure* of education at home and school, with an eye to fitting the medium to the message.

Today we have a marvelous opportunity to schoolproof our children. The work is not that hard— in fact, it's exciting! All it takes is real love, and a determination to put our children *first,* before our projects and plans. The easy way of dumping them into the cheapest and most accessible educational setup turns out to be harder in the end. The harder way, educating ourselves so we can educate them, yields the fruit of wonderful relationships and alive, interested students.

You may have learned to hate learning in school. Come, try it again on your own terms. Pass on what you learn. Demand a *real* education for your children. Give them yourself whatever they can't get elsewhere. And God be with you!

FOOTNOTES

Chapter 1: Are Students Human?

[1]Ruth Beechick, *A Biblical Psychology of Learning: How Your Mind Works* (Denver: Accent House, 1982), pp. 7, 20, 12.

[2]*Ibid.*, p. 47.

[3]Susan Schaeffer Macaulay, *For the Children's Sake: Foundations of Education for Home and School* (Westchester, IL: Crossway Books, 1984), p. 55

[4]*Ibid.*, p. 68.

[5]John Holt did say some things that, in the hands of the ideologically inclined, lead directly to child-worshiping.

> What children need is not new and better curricula but *access* to more and more of the real world; plenty of time and space to think over their experiences, and to use fantasy and play to make meaning out of them; and advice, road maps, guidebooks, to make it easier for them to get where they want to go *(not where we think they ought to go)* and to find out what they want to find out. (*Teach Your Own: A Hopeful Path for Education* [New York: Dell Books, 1981], p. 168. Emphasis mine.)

> The school must be a place where people come together to do the things that interest and excite them most . . . The school must not try to *compel* learning. (*Ibid.*, pp. 187-188)

> Struggling with the inherent difficulties of a chosen or inescapable task builds character; merely submitting to superior force destroys it. (*Ibid.*, p. 65)

> The most important question any thinking creature can ask itself is, "What is worth thinking about?" When we deny its right to decide that for itself, when we try to control what it must attend to and think about, we make it less observant, resourceful, and adaptive, in a word, less intelligent, in a blunter word, more stupid. (*Ibid.*, p. 231)

Although John Holt made absolutist statements about how we should never tell children what to learn, he himself was too much of a realist to believe in the ideal of Perfect Freedom at the expense of the way children actually learn in their families. He also said things like,

> Oddly enough, the reactionary view and the romantic liberal view of children are like opposite sides of the same coin. The hard-nosed types say that to fit children for the world we have to beat the badness out of them. The romantic child-worshippers say that in fitting children for the world we destroy most of the goodness in them. One group claims that children are undersized and defective adults; the other, that adults are oversized and defective children. Neither is true. (*Ibid.*, p. 149)

> It would be impossible, even if you wanted to, not to have *some* influence on your children's view of life. (*Ibid.*, p. 62)

It is your right, and your proper business, as parents, to . . . put as much as you can of good into their lives, and keep out as much as you can of bad. (*Ibid.*, p. 64)

We . . . believe that children want to learn about the world, are good at it, and can be trusted to do it with very little adult coercion . (*Ibid.*, p. 67)

Note that Holt did not say children can be trusted to learn all about the world with absolutely *no* adult coercion. He was also against the idea that there is "something wild and precious in children that had to be preserved against the attacks of the world for as long as possible," saying that people had "suffered" from this "notion." (*Ibid.*, pp. 148-149)

As Holt observed, and as his readers informed him, one of children's most powerful motivations is the desire to fit in to adult society. (*Ibid.*, pp. 208-209, 263.) Parents can count on their children picking up the parents' interests. Holt saw this and thought that it was good.

Children do often seem to me like talented barbarians, who would really like to become civilized . . . My overwhelming impression is that basically they [young babies] want to fit in, take part, and do right—that is, do as we do. (*Ibid.*, pp. 147, 149)

[6]*For the Children's Sake*, Principles 4 and 5, p. 61.

Chapter 2: The Learning Game
[1]*For the Children's Sake*, p. 21.
[2]Betty Macdonald, *Mrs. Piggle Wiggle* (New York: J. B. Lippincott Company, 1947), pp. 13-14.
[3]*For the Children's Sake*, p. 39.
[4]*Biblical Psychology of Learning*, pp. 87-88.

Chapter 3: Getting Up to Speed
[1]*Biblical Psychology of Learning*, pp. 55-57.

Chapter 4: Twenty Ways to Present a Lesson
[1]Carole Thaxton and Jessica Hulcey, *KONOS Character Curriculum*,Volume 1 revised (Richardson, TX: KONOS, 1987), p. 12.
[2]Phyllis Schlafly, *Child Abuse in the Classroom* (Westchester, IL: Crossway Books, 1986), p. 85, 147, 406. This book is a collection of testimonies given before the U. S. Department of Education on the matter of proposed regulations to implement the Protection of Pupil Rights Amendment. Some of the fun activities parents and teachers reported seeing in sex ed classes:

• In my son's 5th grade Health class, all questions were answered without regard to a moral right and wrong. Homosexuality was presented as an alternative lifestyle. Sexual activity among 5th graders was not discouraged . . .

I was present when a plastic model of female genitalia with a tampon insert was passed around to the boys so they might understand how tampons fit. Birth control pills were also passed around and explained. Anal intercourse was described. At no time was there any mention of abstinence as a desirable alternative for 5th graders.

Testimony of Rev. Ronald Watson, p. 85.

• (From a suggested assignment for junior and senior high students throughout the State of Michigan):

"First ask the students to relax, feel comfortable, and close their eyes. Then ask them to fantasize and design a form of birth control that they would enjoy using . . .

Next, ask students to share their designs out loud, noting differences and good ideas. The various designs may elicit much laughter."

"Another brazen example of an attempt at Behavior Modification taken from the same federally-funded manual [*Preparing Professionals for Family Life and Human Sexuality Education*]:"

Vocabulary Brainstorming:

(a) Divide the class into groups of five or six. Select one word or phrase and then have each group list as many synonyms as it can in three to five minutes. Use words such as penis, vagina, intercourse, breast.

(b) Now, rearrange the class into couples and ask that they engage in a conversation for three minutes, trying to use as many of the words on the list as possible."

This manual also asked teachers to develop "values education dilemmas, case studies, or role plays" on subjects such as "boys and girls seeing one another naked," "a teenager's abortion," and "a woman leaving her husband and child."

Testimony of Barbara Powell, pp. 147-148.

• The New York City Board of Education has just published a new Sex Education Program (SEP) . . . One of SEP's major teaching tactics is role-playing, that is, getting pupils of every age to act out roles in various psychological situations. It is a powerful form of psychotherapy. SEP requires pupils to act out these situations: (1) pretend your parents are getting a divorce; (2) pretend you are having a conflict with your parents; (3) pretend someone you know is pregnant; discuss the options she has to choose from "including teenage marriage, adoption, single parenthood, foster care, extended family, abortion"; (4) pretend your boyfriend tells you he has syphilis or gonorrhea.

Testimony of Phyllis Schlafly, p. 407.
[3]*For the Children's Sake*, p. 17.

Chapter 6: Twenty Ways to Show and Tell

[1]*For the Children's Sake*, p. 64.
[2]See Phyllis Schlafly's *Child Abuse in the Classroom* for hundreds of pages of documentation and information about how kids are deliberately programmed like this in the public schools.

Chapter 7: Multiply and Conquer

[1]Unknown to most Americans, the United States has agreed to let the Soviets work with us in the development of curricula and teaching materials for elementary and secondary schoolchildren. The purpose of this agreement is to restructure the education of American children.

Chapter I of this on-going saga took place in Moscow on October 24-29, 1985 when the Carnegie Corporation, with the prior approval of the U. S. Department of State and National Security advisers, entered into negotiations to work with the Soviets in the development of curricula and teaching materials for elementary and secondary schoolchildren.

Impossible? Far-fetched? Way out? No, that's exactly what happened . . .

Discussions resulted in an agreement two weeks later that was signed by the Carnegie Corporation with the Soviet Institute of Informatics. The agreement calls for the Soviets and the Americans jointly to develop and test computer software for use in U. S. elementary schools, and to restructure the curriculum and teaching methods of our early elementary grades through the use of computers . . .

Chapter II of the saga took place at the Geneva Conference on November 21, 1985 when Secretary of State George Shultz signed a 41-page General Agreement with the Soviet Government covering a broad range of exchanges and cooperative projects in the education, scientific and cultural fields. The *Washington Post* of November 26, 1985 quoted the agreement as calling for "cooperation in the development of educational exchanges and software for elementary and secondary school instruction."

But would they use this software to control our kids? You bet they would. Following up this modest proposal, Carnegie Corporation has been working on plans to (1) test all students nationally to determine their values and beliefs and family background and (2) design a one-size-fits-all computer curriculum for all states of the Union. Plans are also in the works for standardized nationwide teacher certification. All this is directed towards the explicitly-stated goal of changing children's goals and attitudes.

"Will We Let the Soviets Teach Our Schoolchildren?," *Phyllis Schlafly Report*, September 1987. Get your own copy of this report by sending $5 to Phyllis Schlafly Report, Box 618, Alton IL 62002.

[2]Edward V. Rickenbacker, *Rickenbacker: An Autobiography* (Englewood Cliffs, NJ: Prentice-Hall, 1967), pp. 31-32.

[3]*For the Children's Sake*, pp. 29-30.

[4]Richard Mitchell, *The Graves of Academe* (Boston: Little, Brown & Company, 1984), pp. 225-226.

[5]Allan Bloom, *The Closing of the American Mind* (New York: Simon and Schuster, 1987), p. 58.

Chapter 8: Educational Clutter's Last Stand

[1]*Instructor* magazine, February 1988, "A+ Schools," p. 32; "Read-iculous Read-a-thon," pp. 108-110; "George Washington Hat Wig" and "Communication with Big Feet," p. 117.

[2]Don Aslett, *Clutter's Last Stand* (Cincinnati: Writer's Digest Books, 1984), p. 41.

Chapter 10: Learning that Fits

[1]"Data from 525 mental health clinics in twenty-four states indicated that more than twice as many boys than girls were brought to these clinics . . . 70 percent of all children in special education are boys." Part of the reason is that boys mature more slowly physically and verbally. Another great part of the reason is that boys' natural behavior is not tolerated in school. According to scholarly studies of the way teachers treat boys and girls,

> Student teachers tended to respond to boys and girls according to preferences they considered appropriate for each sex. For example, they gave higher ratings to the most rigid and conforming children—unlikely behavior for boys far more than girls . . . Teachers also appear more threatening in the preschool to boys than to girls.

Raymond S. and Dorothy N. Moore *et al.*, *School Can Wait* (Provo, UT: Brigham Young University Press, 1979), pp. 179, 183, 185.

[2]An (unfortunately typical) horror story that shows how schools use grades as whips to coerce attendance, rather than as honest assessment devices:

> This is my second year to home school our two daughters, Christy, 15 and Amy, 10 . . .
>
> Christy was in the 8th grade. Unlike Amy, Christy was an honor roll student. But this was a very difficult year for her; there were not only some new teachers, but also a new high school principal. Christy would bring home so much homework that she would work on it from the time she got home until late in the night. She barely had time to eat supper. She became a very irritable and nervous young lady, which was very unlike Christy.

During Christmas vacation she came down with the flu and was still sick when school resumed. After being sick for two weeks the headaches started. There were times she acted better, but she always seemed worse when school was mentioned. Christy's best friend always brought her homework to her. It was piling up by leaps and bounds. I couldn't believe how much work they assigned the kids! I thought to myself, "My gosh, she'll NEVER catch up!" . . .

Report cards came at the end of the 3rd quarter, and my husband and I went to the parent-teacher conference. I couldn't believe Christy's grades—they were all "I's" and "F's"! Was this a JOKE? We went from room to room to ask each teacher how Christy could have made such grades. I knew for a fact that she had made up all of her homework. We were told she missed too much school, and that participation [read: having your body in the classroom] counts as a large percentage of her grades. It really didn't MATTER that she had made up the work! We went to the principal's office and asked HIM how Christy's grades could be so bad. Well, he gave us the biggest line of how Christy's grades were just low because she missed so much school, but for Christy not to dwell on the past but to look forward to the upcoming 4th quarter. Christy's self-esteem hit an all-time low when she looked at the report card through tears streaming down her face. I felt so badly for her, after all those hours she had spent on that homework.

The next day we got a letter from the Juvenile Office. The principal had turned Christy in for missing so many days of school. I was enraged, to think that the smiling, two-faced man had stood there and told us for Christy not to worry while he had called the Juvenile Officer for truancy! We told the Juveniile Officer that Christy had doctor's excuses for her absences and he seemed totally unaware of that!

"Readers Respond," *Heart of America Report*, November 1987, p. 3. A publication of Families for Home Education, 1525 W. Lexington, Independence, MO 64052.

Chapter 12: Godliness with Content

[1]The uproar at Stanford University about which books, if any to require as core readings in the Western Culture course for freshmen ably illustrates this. Blacks want black authors. Feminists want feminist authors. The embattled professors of English who still somehow prefer the great classics to modern twaddle and propaganda are barely able to defend their position— even though Allan Bloom's *The Closing of the American Mind*, which vigorously recommends a return to the Great Books was the number one bestseller on the *New York Times* booklist for months. Humanists have let the special-interests cat out of the bag, and now the homosexuals and minorities and feminists are eating humanistic culture alive.

Stephen Goode, "Read All About It," *Insight*. March 7, 1988, pp. 58-60.

[2]*For the Children's Sake*, p. 137.

INDEX